Praise for *Creating and Sustaining a Thriving Reiki Practice*

Inspiring. Dedicated. Contagious. Three qualities of the excellent teacher that Deb Karpek exudes. Yes, read this book if you want to be inspired about the gifts that Reiki can bring to your life. Also read this book if you want a model of dedication to living a fulfilling life of purpose. But most of all, read this book if you really want to succeed in starting a profession as a Reiki practitioner and teacher. Deb has it all: a track record of success, the ability to communicate what needs to be done in detail and an infectious quality that convinces you to do it. I have witnessed this first hand with her Reiki students. Be prepared to transform your life and livelihood.
      ~ Jim Morningstar, PhD, Director, Transformations Incorporated

In the work of Deb Karpek, a positive and passionate new voice emerges in the field of spiritually-inspired businesses. By sharing her courageous journey to love for herself, Deb proves that a business inspired by a quest for peace of heart and mind and grounded with solid and practical business savvy can indeed be profitable.
      ~ Sunday Larson, Author and Story Mentor, Sedona, AZ

Deb Karpek is the embodiment of Spirit in action! As her student, she has taught me what it means to be a Reiki Master/Teacher, and that is a constant surrender to the Reiki energy so that it masters you. She has taught me this through the way she lives her life, by journeying within oneself to reach truth, unconditional love and authentic presence. Meeting Deb has changed the course of my life. Her mentoring and guidance gave me the courage to leave my career and create my own thriving Reiki practice.
      ~ Rhiana Tehan, Holy Fire Usui and Karuna Reiki Master/Teacher

Deb wants others to succeed and has been an excellent mentor to me. The lessons she has taught me in and out of the classroom are invaluable. Her gentle, yet straightforward manner is authentic. She freely shares with you her experiences, and while she has always encouraged me to do what feels right for me, she nudges me out of my comfort zone. Her mantra, "Do It Afraid," is one I now apply to my own life.

Through the gift of Reiki and Deb's guidance, I have started my own Reiki practice. Not only do I feel that the education and training I received from Deb has assisted with this accomplishment, but the example she has set in her practice has guided me as well. The time she takes with her clients, her passion for sharing Reiki with others, and her professionalism, wit and humor are all qualities I try to incorporate into my own practice.
      ~ Theresa Toporsh, Reiki Master/Teacher

Wow, wow, wow. Love the book! Full of great tips and suggestions! I am already incorporating it into my practice! I will be gifting my Reiki Masters with the book at my classes, because that's exactly what they'll need to start their businesses. She goes over several issues I had myself, when I was just starting out and I would have loved to have had the information that is available in this book. Big thumbs up! Great Job, Deb!
~ Brenda Ault, Karuna Holy Fire Reiki Master, Certified Shaman and BodyTalk Practioner, owner of Namaste Moments.

This book is a one of those gems, an honest and practical how to book. She speaks with clarity encouraging the reader, answering questions you may have thought of and those you may not have thought of. This book is not just for those interested in Reiki but for anyone contemplating creating change in their life. Her voice is true and it feels as if she is in the room with you as a friend and mentor.
~ Kristin Gillan RN, MS , Interspiritual Minister, Colorpuncture Practitioner

I love to read & love any kind of metaphysical or self help book. However, when I started a list of "to do's" while reading I knew this was different. I have pages highlighted to use for reference. It was reassuring when I realized I had already been doing some of Deb's suggestions. It felt good to have confirmation that I was on the right track. I have incorporated some other of the suggestions into my practice and they feel natural. As I'm glancing back through it, I realize I'll need to re-read it and I plan to purchase these as gifts for all the Reiki Masters I teach. It's a wonderful reference guide for anyone on the Reiki path or anyone who is starting a business as a small holistic practitioner. Deb writes in a friendly easy style that is easy to read and feels more like you are sitting down to a cup of tea and chatting.
~ Chellie Kammermeyer

Deb Karpek's book is fantastic! It is not just for Reiki practitioners, but applies to anyone starting their own small business. Deb's experiences in starting her own Reiki practice can be transferred to many different types of businesses, but particularly to anyone in a healing profession. She gives very practical tips on marketing and working through the fear and doubt that can come up when venturing out on your own. I highly recommend this book!
~ Laurie Ozbolt, Spiritual Director, Soaring Hearts

The Reluctant Reiki Master's

Step-by-Step Guide to

Creating & Sustaining

a

Thriving Reiki Practice

**Forthcoming books by Deb Karpek
in the Reluctant Reiki Master Series**

*Illuminations—Keys to Bringing Your
Reiki Practice to the Light*
(a condensed version of this book,
Creating & Sustaining a Thriving Reiki Practice)

Who Do You Think You Are? (memoir)

Illuminating Reiki Journal

Thriving Practice Workbook

The Reluctant Reiki Master's
Step-by-Step Guide to

Creating & Sustaining

a

Thriving Reiki Practice

Deb Karpek

 RADIANT HEART PRESS
Milwaukee, Wisconsin

The author is grateful to *Reiki News Magazine* and Reiki Rays blog, where some of the material in this book first appeared in a different form.

Published by
Radiant Heart Press
An imprint of HenschelHAUS Publishing, Inc.
Milwaukee, Wisconsin
www.henschelhausbooks.com

ISBN: 978159598-462-3
E-ISBN: 978159598-463-0
Library of Congress Control Number: 2016934608

Publisher's Cataloging-In-Publication Data
(Prepared by The Donohue Group, Inc.)

Names: Karpek, Deb.
Title: The reluctant Reiki master's step-by-step guide to creating & sustaining a thriving Reiki practice / Deb Karpek.
Other Titles: Creating & sustaining a thriving Reiki practice
Description: Milwaukee, Wisconsin : Radiant Heart Press, an imprint of HenschelHAUS Publishing, Inc., [2016] | Includes bibliographical references.
Identifiers: LCCN 2016934608 | ISBN 978-1-59598-462-3 | ISBN 978-1-59598-463-0 (ebook)
Subjects: LCSH: Reiki (Healing system)--Practice. | Karpek, Deb--Career in alternative medicine. | Healers. | New business enterprises. | Success in business.
Classification: LCC RZ403.R45 K37 2016 (print) | LCC RZ403.R45 (ebook) | DDC 615.8/52--dc23

Printed in the United States of America

For Hoss

Table of Contents

SECTION ONE:
Reiki Finds You When You Need It
and It Gives You What You Need

SECTION TWO:
Do It Afraid

SECTION THREE:
We Teach Best What We Most Need To Learn

Introduction

This book is for the Reiki professional who is thinking about or ready to start a Reiki practice. I will share with you what I've learned and how I created and nurtured a successful Reiki practice. You will learn why I call myself the "Reluctant Reiki Master" and how I Did It Afraid (so you can, too). At the end of each chapter there is a checklist for you to begin your work. Think of it as a blueprint—one that you will personalize. It's a way for you to get started. The goal of this book is to help you to create and sustain your own successful Reiki practice, using examples of my experiences.

Baring All

I love that I am able to mentor my students. I've been doing it for years, and that is how this book was born. Many of the questions I've been asked by my students became the foundation for this book. From the negative thoughts and fearful emotions, to the nuts and bolts of creating a practice, it's all here. I wish I'd had a book like this when I started my practice. I had to slog through without much support and I made many mistakes. I've learned a lot and am here to share that learning with you.

So much of this stuff is not talked about, especially the fear, insecurity, and mistakes made when starting a Reiki practice. I want to give you an honest portrayal of what I went through on my journey. It is my wish that this book helps to allay your fears, motivates you to Do It Afraid, and allows you to feel all of the feelings that you put into your Reiki practice. Know that it is okay to feel like you can't do it.

Know that it is okay to think you don't measure up. Know that it is okay to be jealous of your fellow Reiki professionals. These are feelings that need to come up, so they can be healed. And I really believe that unless we allow ourselves to experience all of these feelings and deal with them we won't really be successful. Perhaps superficially, but not in wholeness.

I Did It My Way

This is how I did it. It is my experience, in my voice, what worked for me. Find *your own* way to make it work. I did what I did when I needed to do it. I had somewhat of a plan but most of it was swept up in choice, change and synchronicity. If you had told me 10 years ago that I would be living the life I am now, I would not, could not have believed you. And yet, here I am.

Think about your experiences with Reiki. I am fond of the saying "Reiki finds you when you need it and it gives you what you need." I have needed and gotten many different things from Reiki over the years. This is what makes Reiki and the healing that comes from it so unique. Be open to what Reiki has to teach *you*.

You Can Do It

It's important to have a blueprint. Let this book be that blueprint. It may help you to see what I've overcome on the way to learning all of this. Many of you may feel you are not up to the task. You are! Many of you may feel like you really aren't Reiki material. You are! Trust me. I felt the same way at one time and was able to transcend that, moving forward one day at a time. I had someone say to me the other day, "Why would anyone come to me?" I know that feeling well. I thought it many times, even after years of a successful practice. That's our ego and our fear speaking and I am here to help you transcend that. I went though it so you don't have to, and I can show you the way.

What Do You Bring to the Table?

So how did I do it? To answer truthfully, even though I had no experience as a small business owner, was scared to death to do this, and felt woefully inadequate and untrained, it really never occurred to me I would fail. I don't mean to sound arrogant, but I've always had a vision of my practice being successful. I believed that despite the fear and insecurity I could do it. I had 30-plus years of working in corporate America under my belt where I soaked up a lot of wisdom and business practices, so I just did it, one step at a time.

How will you begin? What do you have to bring to the table? My years of corporate experience laid the foundation for me. I knew business practices, was organized, and knew how to work independently and in groups. I was a go-getter. These skills were very useful in creating my practice. What are your skills? What has life taught you? What are you good at that you can use in your practice?

If it scares you to think of having a practice, think of it as a new job, another thing that you can do. If you were being interviewed for this job of creating your Reiki practice what experience do you have that will help you succeed? Think about your strengths and successes and apply them to this new job. I found it easier to think of it this way in the beginning rather than imagining the huge task of creating something new. It is really just another job! That took the pressure off and gave me some clarity.

Reiki is the Gift That Keeps on Giving

On some level I also understood that the Reiki flowed through me, and not from me. So even though I felt inadequate to begin my business I knew that by doing Reiki it would help to heal me. My job would help me to succeed. Does that make sense? I knew that every time I gave Reiki I'd get Reiki.

Every time I gave an attunement, I'd get an attunement. I assumed, correctly, that I'd be bringing in more light on a daily basis. And with that light I would not only grow stronger as a teacher and practitioner but I would also heal those things that lead to my self-sabotage. I also understood that I could send Reiki to my practice and ask it to help me grow, both personally and professionally. So I did. And guess what? It worked. Use your Reiki to help you succeed every single day. It is the gift that keeps on giving.

Believe in Yourself and Keep Moving Forward

For so many years, I felt that no one would be interested in what I had to say, so I did not write, at least not for anyone to see. I had boxes and boxes of journals down in my basement, writings of me screaming to be heard, most of them doused with red wine stains. They were sloppy, drunken tales of woe and self-pity-my sad, sappy poetry and stories of longing and rejection. Then I got sober and started writing to empty myself out. A book I found offered up writing prompts and I was off! Each day I wrote a new chapter of my new life, purging the old, and getting to know my new, sober self.

As I improved, so did my writing. At about the six-month sobriety mark I submitted a story comparing those six months to a bike ride I had just taken. To my surprise and astonishment, it was published. A *Chicken Soup for the Recovering Soul* story followed and I began to publish monthly articles in a women's recovery newsletter.

Introduction

Women started contacting me, telling me they could relate to my stories. Again, I was surprised. When I write I don't think about the reader. If I did I'd never submit. I was too insecure and worried about judgment.

A few years ago, I started writing for *Reiki News Magazine*. I began publishing a couple of articles a year. This was a dream come true. Years earlier I had submitted something that was rejected. I took it very personally, and let it speak to my insecurities about my writing. I wasn't good enough. I wasn't a real Reiki person. Who did I think I was?

I persevered, submitted more stores and after a while I began getting published. I heard from many readers, emails telling me how much people enjoyed my stories. They could relate and they thanked me for my honesty.

So now I am embarking on a book. I always tell my students how Reiki brings up our stuff. And this book is bringing up my stuff! Oh my goodness! So I keep my mantra front and center: DO IT AFRAID! I am not going to get sucked in to the old fears, insecurities and comparisons. No, I am NOT my teacher. I am me, with my own unique stories and experiences. It is enough. I am enough.

Which is exactly the opposite of how I've felt most of my life. For many, many years I would hear *Who do you think you are?* from my parents when I tried to embark on something new, creative, or different. Who do I think I am? Well, jeez, I'm me, trying something new. Nope! *We don't do that! You don't have the talent or the smarts. Be satisfied with what you have.*

Most of my childhood I heard *Don't take risks! Don't do anything foolish! Stay safe! Stay inside that box!* That may have been my parent's story and experience, but it wasn't mine. I was a good girl with the heart and soul of a rebel, so often I'd try something new and get shot down. After years of hearing *Who do you think you are?* I began to believe that maybe they were right. Maybe I was just average, and maybe I should just stop trying. So I did.

For many years I let myself believe that average was okay and that I just wanted to be like everyone else. But energy doesn't lie and it never felt right. It wasn't me. I rebelled, but it was against myself. I hid my light, covered it up so I would seem "normal." I craved attention but instead of being who I was, I pretended to be someone else. I acted out and got the attention but not in the way I wanted it. I let myself get lost in the darkness for too long.

Don't do this. Allow your light to shine. Reiki helped me to turn my light back on. Who do I think I am? Well, I am no longer the Reluctant Reiki Master! I recognize the fear and move ahead, Doing It Afraid, which transcends the fear and propels me forward. I am happy and grateful to have met Reiki.

I was told by a teacher of mine that I have the ability to straddle both worlds—the esoteric world of Reiki energy healing and the nuts and bolts of the business part of it. I learned a lot during my time in the corporate world and I have brought that prior experience to my Reiki practice. I believe it is why I was successful at the many left brained aspects of running a Reiki business. Things like marketing, organizing, websites, correspondence, presentations, etc. came very easy to me. I equally love both sides of the business as it gives me the ability to use all of my skill sets. It's a very satisfying combination and keeps things interesting. All of those years of sitting in on the endless meetings, taking minutes, I was soaking up a lot of wisdom that I now use in my practice. I'm so grateful to have had these diverse work experiences.

So again, I ask you to examine your skills, experience and abilities and integrate them into creating your own Reiki practice. Let me lay the foundation so you can build your own house, your very own successful Reiki practice.

Introduction

And lastly, no one can do it for you. Sooner or later you are going to have to make the leap-to practicing, to teaching, to having a business. Each and every one of these things can be big and scary but the only way you are going to do them is to do them, even if you are afraid. It's just fear, it's not real.

Talking about it helps us to get there but after a certain point it becomes a crutch. Talking about it is not doing it. Thinking about it is not doing it. Making plans but not following through is not doing it. Stop talking about it and do it.

Once you do it you will wonder why you waited so long. And if you are unable to make the leap ask yourself why? Ask Reiki to help you discover what is at the bottom of this inability to move forward. Fear? Insecurity? Not deserving? Finances? Family? Figure out what it is and deal with it.

You might ask, "What if I fail?" What if you don't? And let's indulge your fear and the worst-case scenario happens and you do fail. OK. You failed. At least you did it. You can always try again or try something else but you will have the satisfaction of having done it. That's something. As opposed to keeping on wishing, being the victim, not taking your turn, living in that land of longing. Don't let life pass you by. Jump! The net will appear. Trust this. The only difference between those who succeed and those who do not is that those who succeed take the risk and do it. It's really that simple.

Thank you for choosing this book. It is Book One in the Reluctant Reiki Master Series. Book Two, *Illuminations, Keys to Bringing your Reiki Practice to the Light*, a condensed version of this book, is coming soon, followed by *Who Do You Think You Are?* my memoir. There will be an *Illuminating Reiki Journal* and a *Thriving Practice Workbook*, so you can keep track of your progress as you begin to create your Reiki practice. It is my wish that these products help you on your Reiki path. Good luck and don't forget to use your Reiki.

SECTION ONE

Reiki Finds You
When You Need It
and
It Gives You
What You Need

What is Reiki?

Rei = Universal Life Force   *Ki* = Energy

Defining Reiki is difficult for me. It works on so many levels: mentally, physically, emotionally and spiritually. It gives us what we need when we need it and because we all need different things at different times, it provides on many levels. I could go on and on but the best way to really learn Reiki is by exploring its energy: getting it, or doing it, to your self or another. And don't worry if you don't feel anything. Keep doing it. It always works and never does any harm. In time you will feel its presence in your life. Trust.

That being said, I'll give you some definitions to help you to try to understand. Reiki is Universal Life Force Energy-the energy that surrounds us. Another definition I use in teaching is from William Rand, founder of the International Center for Reiki Training. "Reiki is a Japanese technique for stress reduction and relaxation that also promotes healing." I also like to say that Reiki strengthens the body's natural ability to heal itself, on all levels, physical, emotionally, mentally, and spiritually. These are the descriptions I use when asked. And it never seems to adequately cover what it is.

It's such a big, yet gentle, energy. If you haven't had a session yet, get one. If you are attuned to Reiki, give it to yourself. Get to know it. Be patient and give it time to get to know you. I have a client who says it took her three or four sessions before her body got used to it and let more in. I like that.

One of the best definitions, and my favorite is "This is Reiki. Put your hands on the person and get out of the way." Done. Boom. That's it. Class over. So simple yet so true.

Let Reiki tell you what it is. Let Reiki teach you. Give, receive, ask. Reiki will tell you. However, when pressed I like to say I believe Reiki to be God's energy, the divine light from Source.

I can teach you the business of Reiki, the logistics of building and keeping a business; allow Reiki to teach you about Reiki.

Is Reiki for You?

Of course it is! You would not have picked up this book if it weren't calling you in some way. It is said that everyone has the ability to do Reiki. Not everyone may be called to do it and not all those who are called may heed that call, but I honestly believe that anyone can do Reiki.

Reiki is for everyone. I teach that we are already wired for it. It is there, waiting for activation. As the teacher, when I give an attunement, I am like the electric company, turning you on, flipping the switch. That is the activation! You are now attuned. You are now a channel. You are now filled with the bright light of that Universal Life Force energy that Reiki is. Reiki is light. Reiki is love. Let it guide you and teach you.

After the Level One attunement, you will be able to give yourself Reiki, your friends, your family, your pets, your plants—anyone and anything. Yes, you are a channel. With each subsequent attunement, your channel grows larger and it continues to grow the more you use it. It never diminishes, even if you never, ever use it. You will always be a channel. The more Reiki you do the wider your channel becomes. And remember, Reiki flows through you, not from you. I feel this really takes the pressure off. It's not you!

I've had many students take my classes who had no interest in teaching or practicing professionally. Know that you do not have to. Use Reiki as your own personal discovery tool. For me Reiki was the key that opened a door to unknown worlds. So many things changed for me after I began getting Reiki attunements. I like to say that we don't know what we don't know and that is certainly true with regards to Reiki. I had no idea what was in store for me. So if you are being called but are not sure you want to practice or teach, follow the Reiki path anyways. At the very least you will raise your vibration and acquire some new tools. And who knows? You may surprise yourself and one day practice and/or teach. Be open to the miracles that Reiki brings.

When I took my first class I assumed I was there for my own personal healing. That is true. Reiki heals us first and foremost, even if that is not our intention when we take the class. I also (wrongly) assumed I'd never need to go any further than Level One. At the end of the day the other students were making plans for the Level Two class they would take. I demurred. I had no intention to go any further. Yet when I heard the call to continue, I listened, even if I did not understand why.

We all have different reasons why we start, and I've since learned they are never what we think they are. The beautiful thing about Reiki is it will give you what you need, when you need it. It's there for you, just waiting for you to tap into its beautiful energy. Now I knew none of this—again, this is spoken from the vantage point of being involved with Reiki for many years—but it is true. It is waiting for you. It is so excited that you heeded the call. You listened and you will be rewarded with the changes it will bring to you. Reiki is our own personal GPS—guiding us back to who we really are. It gives us back to us. Amen!

The Call—My Path to Reiki
From Reluctant to Seasoned

My wish in sharing with you my path to Reiki is that it may help you in yours. Perhaps you will see yourself in the many situations I have experienced. I like to think that I am helping you to lay your foundation. Know it's ok to make mistakes, to fail, to feel the fear (but Do It Afraid). Set your intention and get out there. Let go of concerns and trust the process. Keep moving forward.

A few months ago a patient at the cancer center where I used to work asked me how I found Reiki. When I told her my story she said, "Nothing like a calling!" My call was subtle yet persistent. I'm glad it came in slow and steady, because it allowed me to listen. Had it come in fast and hard I might have run away. I almost didn't know what was happening to me, yet I had an intuitive sense to keep on going.

I have heard and believe that many are called but not all heed the call. I was called when I wasn't particularly looking for it, but Reiki grabbed hold of me and kept at me until I started my formal training, and beyond. It stayed with me through all of my levels and it stayed with me while I went out into the world and began my practice. All of these years later it's still with me, as I created another practice in a new state, set up a Reiki program at a cancer center and wrote this book. It's always here with me. I just need to remember to ask it and use it. It's that simple.

Meeting Reiki

I never meant for this to happen; it was never planned. I fought it in the beginning and sometimes tried to run from it but it always pulled me back in. For a long time I called myself the Reluctant Reiki Master because I resisted it so much. It took a while but I eventually surrendered to it.

I discovered Reiki at a Women's Wellness Conference in the spring of 2000. It's odd that I was even there. I had recently quit drinking and had a lot of time on my hands. Saturday mornings usually found me in bed, hung over and remorseful. Now that I was sober I had plenty of time to venture out and try new things.

I went alone, another oddity. None of my friends were willing to fork over the $75 for the daylong event. So I gathered up my courage and off I went. I felt so adult as I sat in the morning welcome session, sharing breakfast with a table of seven strangers. I was feeling shy and insecure but I "Did It Afraid," a newly discovered mantra, and one I still employ to this day.

The first breakout session I attended was "Alternative Healing Methods." Honestly, I had no interest in any of this. I went because it was the only one that had any space left. I had waited so long to register most of the sessions were full. I considered hanging out in the shopping area but something lured me into that room.

A dozen different speakers of various alternative modalities took turns speaking. About half way through, a nurse from a local hospital took the podium to speak to the group about Reiki. All of a sudden I perked up. I sat up straighter in my chair and began to really pay attention. Prior to this I was drifting, thinking again of hitting up the shopping area of the conference. Suddenly I was completely absorbed. I remember thinking *I'm going to do this* and then laughing to myself thinking *No way*. This feeling, this paying attention to Reiki, ignited my passion. It burns brightly to this day.

After the session I went up to the Reiki woman and spoke with her. I was excited to learn more about this wonderful new thing called Reiki. She was very gracious with her time and generous with her resources. She gave me her contact information and invited me to a Reiki Share at the hospital. I became a student of Reiki, just like that.

It was so confusing! At the time, I was a conference planner, a very black-and-white profession. Reiki is gray, very, very gray and I found it difficult to understand. I was not comfortable not understanding it. I went from book to book and website to website, growing more confused with each attempt to get it. I'd sit for hours in bookstores reading, yearning to understand.

My Own Energy

In retrospect I see I have always had the ability to feel energy. My husband used to tell people that "my idle was higher than most" when what I think he was really saying was that I had a lot of energy coursing through me. But because I never thought in terms of energy I didn't understand it. Instead I was called "hyper" and thought of this as a bad thing.

I exercised a lot, not so much for my body, but to burn off this excess energy. I believe I drank in the evenings for the same reason. I had so much energy and didn't know what to do with it. Not long after I quit drinking I discovered Reiki and it has really helped me to balance my energies. I have had a relatively smooth recovery and I owe that to Reiki. Getting and giving Reiki keeps me in the flow. It has helped me on so many levels and I am so grateful for discovering it, especially when I did. I believe it saved me.

So I had all of this information in my head about Reiki and it just would not leave me alone; it kept poking at me. I thought about it all of the time, I dreamed about it and I was starting to think it might be time to get a session.

One day I was at the local health food store reading the bulletin board while waiting in line for the rest room. One card on this board of many seemed to be glowing, calling out to me. It belonged to a Reiki Master. I put the card in my pocket and carried it around for a few months. I used it like a worry stone and soon it grew soft and faded. I thought about calling but was too afraid. What if this person could read my mind? What if she put a spell on me? The pull to Reiki was there but my fear was stronger and it held me back.

My First Reiki Experience

A few weeks later I was at a health fair and there was a woman doing ten-minute Reiki samplers. I sat down in her chair and in a matter of minutes I felt transformed! I was feeling ill and out of sorts that day. I had been arguing with my husband and I felt crabby and mean. Sitting in the chair I began to tingle and I could feel the energy flowing through me.

Even though we were in a crowded room with many people and bright lights, I relaxed immediately as a warm glow began to fill my body. The ten minutes flew by and when I got up from her chair I felt so light and free. I felt loving and lovable. This feeling stayed with me for the entire day. I was convinced I needed more and I called the Reiki Master on the card I had been carrying around and set up an appointment.

I had a spectacular first session! It was and still is one of the most amazing experiences of my life. It's so hard to put into words, the feelings ran so deep. Driving home I felt wrapped up in a bubble of love. This session led to more and eventually I began to study Reiki in earnest. I loved how it made me feel and I wanted to know more about this mysterious thing called Reiki.

The Call—My Path to Reiki

Reiki Level One

It wasn't long before I called a teacher I had met at an information session. She had a Level One class starting in a few weeks and I signed up. At the time I doubted I would actually go, but I was doing my best to Do It Afraid. At this point in my journey I signed up for many things, but would usually cancel the day of the event, due to fear and insecurity. A writing teacher I know told me I had cancelled so many workshops that it paid for a couple of scholarships. No kidding!

The day of my Reiki One class I remember sitting in front of the home of the teacher, debating whether or not I should go in. I was so scared! What was going to happen in there? How was it going to change me? Did I really need this? My mind was working overtime, but in my heart, I knew this was the right thing for me to do. I made a conscious decision to Do It Afraid. This would be the first of many times I would not give in to my fear, to my mental monkey mind, and go with what was in my heart. In retrospect I see that I was trusting the Reiki energy, even though I wasn't entirely conscious of doing that. I just called it Doing It Afraid.

After receiving my Level One attunement, I wanted to work on everyone! The Reiki passion ran deep. I ordered a table and even before it came I worked on family, friends, co-workers, literally anyone I could get my hands on. I loved the feeling of the Reiki flowing through me, the laying of my hands on others, feeling the different energies, learning to discern the subtle differences. I immersed myself in all things Reiki. I felt reborn, enthusiastic, full of love and life. I couldn't get enough! Each night before I went to sleep I practiced the self-healing hand positions. I slept well and woke up refreshed and ready to go.

Despite all of my enthusiasm and love of Reiki at the time I did not see myself going on to Level Two. When my teacher suggested it, I hemmed and hawed. I said I would think about it, but I really didn't see myself going any further. I was going to stay at Level One. My Reiki teacher got married and moved away and I lost touch with her. In a way I was relieved, as I wouldn't have to face those questions any longer.

Reiki Level Two

About six months after I received my first attunement I started thinking about going on to Level Two. I began asking friends and co-workers if they knew a good Reiki teacher and the same name kept coming up. I went to see her for a session. It felt good to receive Reiki again. She had a class coming up in a few weeks and I decided to take it.

Again, the debate in the car on the morning of the class, much like the first time. This time my fear was stronger. My mind was telling me all sorts of scary things, like *who do I think I am, going on to Level Two? I am a fraud, a fake! I can't do this! What if others are more advanced than me? What if they see through me? What if I can't remember the symbols or how to draw them? What if the attunement doesn't take?* I sat there, mired in this swirl of negative thoughts and emotions and almost drove away. I didn't because, again, in my heart, I knew I was going to do this. I knew this was just fear and insecurity and it wasn't real. What was real was in my heart. Again, without realizing it, I was trusting the Reiki energy and I was *Doing It Afraid*.

It was a good day, a good class. I loved the symbols! I felt an immediate connection to them; it seemed I already knew them on some level. I loved drawing them and I couldn't wait to use them. We practiced that day and instead of feeling fearful and insecure, I felt wrapped up in love and I really enjoyed using them. In the past when I'd have to demonstrate something I'd get nervous and sort of fake it but I didn't feel that way. I remember thinking that if I didn't understand or know I'd just ask for help. This was a new way of thinking for me; I never asked for help. I used to see it as a sign of weakness. Instead I felt very comfortable and real practicing the symbols and working on my fellow classmates. I remember not wanting to leave class, to stay in this warm cocoon of Reiki and love.

And then an interesting thing happened after I took the class. I didn't practice. I would tell myself every day that I would and when it came time I'd make up excuses. I stopped the self-healing sessions in the evening and I couldn't bring myself to practice on my friends and family, as I had been doing for the previous six months. People would ask for sessions and I'd make excuses. I took down my table and told my husband to sell it on EBay, that I wasn't going to work on people anymore. He suggested putting it in the basement and waiting a bit to see if I changed my mind. I was sure I wouldn't.

One thing I did do was practice writing the symbols. I loved the feel of them, their shapes, what they meant. I felt an immediate and intimate connection with them. Daily, first thing in the morning I drew them in my journal. I also began to do distant healings. I loved the ritual of it. I'd light a candle and either use a picture or a name written on a piece of paper and send Reiki to my friends in California, Florida, and Massachusetts. I sent Reiki to my brothers across town, to my workspace and co-workers. I enjoyed this very much, but I still couldn't bring myself to work on people. I felt as if I was done with that. I decided to just do distant Reiki. I asked my husband to sell the table. I was done with that part of Reiki.

Reiki Master Practitioner

About six months later, still in this mode, I began thinking about my first Reiki experience. I contacted that Reiki Master and set up another session. I hadn't had one since before my Level Two class and felt I needed one. It was good to see this woman again. She told me she had recently become a Teacher and I shared that I was considering moving on to Master Practitioner. We stayed in contact and I continued to receive treatments from her.

Slowly, I began to practice Reiki again, starting with myself, at night, before I went to bed, as was my ritual. It felt good to have it back in my life. I worked on my husband, as he sat in his recliner, watching television. I asked him to find me another table on EBay. Instead, he brought the table back up from the basement, as he never sold it. He knew me better than I knew myself. The practice sessions began again. It felt great to be doing Reiki again.

In retrospect I believe the reason I stopped practicing was to devote time to the symbols and the distant healing. It wasn't so much fear or resistance as wanting to really immerse myself in these new practices. I'm grateful to have had this time, as I really connected to the symbol usage and distant healing and then was able to integrate it with my practice when it began again. I was beginning to gain some confidence and becoming quite devoted to Reiki.

About six months later, almost a year to the day of my Reiki Level Two class I received my Reiki Master Practitioner attunement, from the woman I received my first full Reiki session from. It seemed symbolic and I am so glad I chose her. This time, as I drove to class, I felt surer of myself and my decision to become a Reiki Master. I could see how I was making some significant changes in my life, as a result of this new energy. I was willing to continue on this path, open to whatever it would bring. There was a tiny part of me that still held my fear but I brushed it aside. My heart knew, and I knew, this was what I was supposed to be doing. No more debates in the car, I was ready!

I felt reborn after the class. I was more comfortable in my own skin, more real, like for the first time I knew who I was and where I was going. I knew that no matter what happened or where I went, or whom I was with, I was connected to this thing called Reiki. I could trust it and it would lead me to where I needed to go. I felt safe. I continued to practice, and loved how it felt to work on others, to work on myself, to be aware of the Reiki energy. I began to meditate and started spending most of my spare time in nature, in the woods. I was beginning to connect to things on a level I never had before. I felt in awe of this new life and was so very grateful. Life was good!

Again, I didn't see myself going any further. At the time I didn't realize that I felt this way after each class, it's only looking back that I notice this pattern. I didn't want to move on to Teacher; I couldn't see myself teaching/attuning others. It wasn't me. I would just continue to practice Reiki on the side.

I set up a Reiki room in my home and filled it with the things I loved. It transformed from a messy home office to a peaceful place of meditation and Reiki. I began to charge my friends and co-workers for sessions; half price, a "friend" rate. Initially I had a hard time with this, as I felt very uneasy with the concept of accepting money for Reiki. After all, it wasn't my job, it was something I loved to do, and besides these were my friends and co-workers. Yet, I'd read enough to know there had to be an exchange. I also knew that it had to do with my issues surrounding money and I had to work on this.

I had a sort of business going for a few months in my new Reiki room, working on friends, family, and co-workers. I was starting to have thoughts about moving beyond my home and out into the community. They were just the teeniest of thoughts and when I'd allow them in I'd be filled with that initial dread and fear. All of those old questions and insecurities would pop into my head. But this time there was something different-a sort of excitement and a knowing that it would happen. There again, in my heart, that knowing! The heart was beginning to take over the head, and I was starting to understand and trust the Reiki energy.

My First Reiki Job

I began my practice in July of 2005. In April of that year I received my Reiki Master Practitioner attunement. It was not my intention to begin my practice that soon, but Reiki had other plans for me.

One day I was at my gym. As I was walking out I noticed a door opening into a dimly lit space. The smell of lavender drifted out and drew me into this room. It was a massage room and as I looked in I had a vision of myself doing Reiki in this room. I knew in a very short amount of time I would be practicing Reiki here. Never mind that there was no Reiki at this gym. That didn't seem to matter. As I stood there, seeing this, knowing this, a friend walked over and asked me what I was doing. I replied "I'm going to do Reiki here," surprising both of us!

I went home and wrote a letter to the owner of the gym, introducing myself, asking if I could come in and talk with him about practicing Reiki there. I included my Reiki resume and wrote up an information sheet on Reiki in case he didn't know what it was. A week later I got a call from the lead massage therapist inviting me in for an interview. She was familiar with Reiki, as her son had just received his Reiki Level One attunement. She was very excited about the possibility of having Reiki at the health club.

The Call—My Path to Reiki

The interview was a huge success. It went on for hours! She agreed that Reiki would be a great addition to the spa and she had many good marketing ideas. I was asked back for a second interview, where I would meet the owner and also do a Reiki session on the therapist. In the past I was always nervous before an interview. However, this time I felt ready and on some level I knew I would be practicing there. It felt so right. The day of the second interview I was offered the job and negotiated a good contract. I started the following week.

Caution

Once I secured the position at the gym the old fears and insecurities reared their ugly heads. *What had I gotten myself into? Am I insane? Who do I think I am? No one is going to come! I'll have to work on strangers! On people I don't know! On men!* That last thought scared the daylights out of me! Outside of my husband and my brothers, I had never worked on a man I didn't know. I wasn't sure I even could. *Oh, my goodness, what have I gone and done? Help!*

I pulled out my old mantra, "Do It Afraid." I hadn't had to use it in a while, but I knew I needed it. While my head raged, my heart calmly told me to do it and it would be okay. Honestly I didn't see how this was possible, but knowing that it worked in the past I listened and trusted. This mantra has helped me for so long in so many ways. Find a mantra that works for *you*. What is the magic phrase that will propel you forward when you feel self-sabotage coming on?

My first order of business was to do two nights of "Reiki Samplers" where I would offer Reiki, for two hours, at 20-minute intervals, free of charge. A sign-up sheet was provided in advance and when I arrived it was full. Oh, no! To say I was terrified is an understatement. I thought I would both throw up and faint and I'd be fired, never to return. So much for my Reiki career!

As I prepped the room and did my meditation, I lost the fear and could not wait to introduce Reiki to this new population. I loved doing it so much, I decided to let the love in, and it just swallowed up the fear and negativity I'd been wallowing in. My first two clients were sisters and they each made appointments for future paying sessions. They both responded very well to the Reiki and I couldn't wait to work on them for longer sessions. Everyone showed up, the night flew by and I was so happy and grateful to have had this opportunity. I felt so lucky! (Note: the two sisters became regular clients of mine. They will always have a special place in my heart, being the first two "strangers" I worked on.)

As a condition of my employment I also had to do community education talks about Reiki. Having never done public speaking I was terrified and actually told the owner that I wasn't going to do it. He reminded me that I had to; it was in my contract. We set up the talks and once again that old hamster wheel of fear started spinning in my brain. Looking back, it amazes me how much fear I had and how it took me so long to learn to trust the Reiki energy. But like everything, it is a process and I had to experience it.

All of the talks were well attended, with a lively discussion period. I gained many clients from these talks and was able to introduce Reiki to a population that had never heard of it. I was asked many challenging questions, so it was a good education for me, although at the time I didn't see it that way. It's always been hard for me to explain Reiki, but in those days I felt I *had* to. If I was unable to "convince" someone I felt like a failure. I no longer feel I have to convince anyone, but rather share what I know. I'd still rather do it than talk about it, but I also really enjoy bringing Reiki to populations that are not familiar with it, so it's important for me to do the talks.

I thought it would take a while for the Reiki sessions to catch on at the gym, but to my surprise and delight I was busy from the start. I worked two half days per week, doing two sessions each day and most of the slots were full. There were a lot of curious folks, people who had heard of Reiki but didn't know where to go to get it, people who came to my talks or samplers and wanted to try it, folks who wanted to release stress, folks who were sick and wanted to have it aid in their healing. I met so many different and interesting people and I continue to work on many of them to this day.

Starting a Reiki Practice in the Community

At about the one-year mark at the gym I began thinking about branching out, working in the community. The gym gig was going well, but I wanted to work with a broader population. I had volunteered at health fairs and had gotten a taste of working with a more diverse client base and wanted more of that. I put the thought out there and then immediately felt panic at leaving my safe nest at the gym. I fit in well there, was part of the team, enjoyed my clients, yet I knew the time to move on to the next level was looming.

Through a contact at the local Chamber of Commerce, I found out about a woman who owned an acupuncture clinic who was looking to sub-lease space. I was given her name and number. I was familiar with her ads; in fact on some level I felt as if I knew her, even though we'd never met. I figured I'd give her a call in a few months, at the end of the summer. I didn't want to start something new quite yet, but when I did I'd contact her.

A few days later I heard a voice telling me to call this woman. This voice was very insistent and kept reminding me to contact her. I was becoming familiar with this voice so I gave in and sent her an email. I figured I did my part, that it would take a while for her to get back to me and I was safe, at least for a bit.

Her call came bright and early the next morning! She said she was about to place an ad to sub-lease space and wanted to meet me before she did this. I agreed to come in that afternoon. All the way to the clinic I told myself why I couldn't do this. *I'm not ready! I couldn't afford it! Where will I get my clients? The gym paid for all of my marketing costs and didn't charge me rent; why would I want to change that?* I decided I'd go in, meet her and leave. I didn't *have* to do anything.

The clinic was seven minutes from my home, in a very good location. Not bad. I walked into the waiting room and felt immediately at home. It was a beautiful space. The owner came out, introduced herself and told me to look around, on my own, and get a feel for the space. She asked me to contact her the next day and let her know if I was interested. I wandered around, liking what I saw.

There were a number of different treatment rooms, but a room in the back was calling to me. I entered the door of this room and I saw myself in it, doing Reiki. Much like my vision at the gym I *knew* I'd be working here, practicing Reiki. It felt right. Before my mental monkey mind could kick into gear and get the best of me I drove directly to the gym, gave my notice and agreed to sub-lease the space. Whew! Heady stuff! The Reiki energy was leading me to my next adventure and I was trusting it! I felt this with all my heart. I was filled with gratitude and awe at this wonderful opportunity.

Reiki Master/Teacher Training in Sedona

Right before I found this space I had been in Sedona, Arizona receiving my Reiki Master/Teacher attunements. I was still in the glow of that experience and I believe the Reiki energy was high; I was very tapped into it. I came home and continued tomeditate and began incorporating what I had learned there into my daily life. I was made aware of the shift my life had taken in the year since I'd become a Reiki Master. I was learning to trust this energy, to listen to that inner voice, to be led by this higher source. I found that I was living a life based on my values, that I was starting to walk the talk. I had to Do It Afraid much less.

Sedona, Arizona is one of my favorite places. It's in the high desert, about two hours north of Phoenix and two hours south of the Grand Canyon. It is a small, eclectic community, filled with locals, seekers, retirees and tourists.

The very first time I visited, in the fall of 1994 I had a vision of us living there. I knew that some day, in some way, we'd make this place our home. I had no idea how this was going to manifest but I believed so strongly in this vision that I trusted. Eighteen years later my vision became a reality. Believe in your dreams and take guided action to make them happen. I am living proof it works

I had a profound spiritual awakening in Sedona in the spring of 2000, when I first began to walk this path of self-discovery. I'd been traveling there a lot since then, tapping into its magical energy, hiking among the beautiful red rocks and getting to know this special place.

After six months of practicing as a Reiki Master I felt ready to move on to the Teacher level. I decided as a gift to myself I would go back to the place I had my awakening and receive it there. I would time it so it would occur on my husband's birthday weekend. I had no idea who to go to or how to even find a teacher, so I went to the Internet, googled "Reiki in Sedona" and up popped a Reiki class! I was excited to see they had Master/Teacher training the exact weekend I had already booked my vacation for! I signed up without a thought. Everything lined up perfectly.

I have to admit I went to that training feeling a bit cocky. Gone was the shivering wreck in the car, debating whether or not I should go in. I couldn't wait to get there! I was hyper with excitement! What's to be afraid of? I was already a Master! I was ahead of the game! I was in Sedona! What could go wrong?

Well...

The training was everything I could hope for and more. My instructors were amazing; they are excellent teachers, beautiful people, and being in this class of ten women was like being wrapped in a Reiki cocoon of love. Even after nine hours each day I didn't want to leave. I could have stayed there forever. Being attuned outside on the balcony facing the red rocks of Sedona was a dream come true. I remember feeling so happy and so full of gratitude, marveling at the changes in my life over the past five years.

That's not to say this training wasn't difficult. In a way it was the most difficult thing I've ever experienced. Parts of myself were revealed to me in those three days that had been so deeply buried I'd barely been aware of them. I say barely because they hovered at the edges of my consciousness, waiting, and they picked that weekend to come out. I felt ripped open, exposed, and raw. I don't think I've ever felt more vulnerable, or cried so much as I did that weekend.

It was scary but in a different way. Instead of Doing It Afraid, I just let myself be. I let myself feel these things and let the thoughts unravel. I didn't try to fake it till I made it. I just was. It felt like a boulder slid off my shoulder and a light was shining on me, in me, all the way through me. I met my inner child the second day. Up to this point I thought this inner child business was just a bunch of hooey. She'd been waiting a long time for me and I finally embraced her, with gratitude and love.

I hiked every morning and things popped into my head, clear as day. I made some big life decisions and followed through on them, even though they seemed like not the right decisions. My heart was screaming out and I was listening. I returned home, exhausted *and* exhilarated, ready to live this new life. I was reborn.

Now armed with all of my training, I began my practice in earnest as a full-time Reiki Master/Teacher. A year at the spa flowed into a year as part of a practice. I was living my dream!

Leaving the Real World

In January of 2006 I had the first flicker of feelings about leaving my job to practice Reiki full time. I shared these feelings in an email with a friend. A month later, the Universe responded to my call and set things in motion.

In February, I was in Florida on vacation with my husband. One night walking on the beach, I *knew* I would be quitting my job by summer. The feeling came in swift and strong and I had no doubt that it would happen. I was afraid but I knew it was time.

I went back to work but didn't have the courage to give my notice. I kept worrying about the money and doing Reiki full time seemed self-indulgent. Then one day I was required to come in on my day off for a staff meeting. I felt angry about this but went in. After being there a few hours, I was told the meeting was cancelled.

This gave me the motivation to walk into my boss's office and give my notice. She felt I was reacting to the situation and didn't take me seriously. I then went to my other boss and gave her my notice as well. My anger at the situation motivated me to do what I'd been wanting to do, what my soul had been aching for. It was just the push I needed. I think having set my intention the Universe was working with me and I was in the flow.

I gave a three-month notice and in the middle of May I went to Sedona and met the people who would become my new Reiki teachers. I took my Master/Teacher training and that changed everything. It jump-started me on this Reiki path and I am forever grateful.

Reiki is My Real Job

So, no job in the "real world," and no guaranteed paycheck and not quite a thriving Reiki practice. What to do? Get on with it! Market! Get my name out there! Do whatever I can to create and sustain my soon to be successful Reiki practice.

My first month in my practice at the acupuncture clinic I saw four clients. Luckily I had a deal with the woman I sub-leased the space from where I paid her a percentage of each client rather than a flat fee for rent. It would take one year for me to get enough clients to pay the flat fee rent.

That year was spent getting the word out about my business. How did I do this? (More detail about all of the below in future chapters.)

I joined networking groups, the Chamber of Commerce, and started doing "trades". I bartered with the people in my clinic-massages, acupuncture and Reiki. I traded services with my hairstylist and others who had things I wanted. Many of these people became the base of my practice and they referred their friends and relatives to me. This clinic was down the street from the gym I just left and several of those clients found me and continued to work with me.

It was a wonderful year of growth and expansion. I worked hard at marketing my practice by creating new business cards, brochures and flyers. I went around the neighborhood and put the flyers on bulletin boards in stores and in mailboxes in the subdivision next to our clinic. All of this hard work paid off and many new clients joined my practice.

My goal was to spend a year at this clinic and if I was successful and still loved it I would then create my own space. I envisioned a healing center, with lots of women coming for classes, retreats and Reiki.

At the year mark my practice had grown to the point where it was no longer feasible to share a space. I had been sharing two rooms with a few other practitioners. This worked for a while but when another practitioner was added to the fold it became a little tight. I took this as a sign to start looking for a space. It was time and I was ready!

The Healing Center is Born

One gorgeous summer day I was in a fine mood, having just had lunch with an old friend. I was on my way to a Reiki appointment, running a bit late, when I heard a voice that said, very clearly, "Deb, turn left." I ignored it. Again, "Deb, turn left." This time I told it, "No, I can't! I'm going to be late. There's all this construction; I don't have time!" Once more, this time loud and forceful "DEB, TURN LEFT NOW!" I turned left.

Driving down the street I was looking for whatever it was I was supposed to be seeing. An office building appeared on my right. It had a sign on the front that said "Rental Inquiries." I knew this was what I was supposed to see. I had been looking for a new space to practice Reiki, as my business was growing. I wrote down the number, drove home and called. I had that feeling of anticipation in my stomach; this was good!

A man answered the phone and told me, indeed, he did have some space for rent. I explained what I needed, just a small room to practice Reiki and he told me he had a 1350-square-foot office that had been most recently a dental practice. There were five treatment rooms, a waiting room, office, bathroom and storage. Way too big, I told him. He asked me what I did and when I told him, he replied "I was thinking of turning that space into a co-operative healing arts space."

I almost fainted! While this was *exactly* the vision I'd had in a dream a year ago, I felt it was much too soon. I also hadn't seen myself sharing space with others; I desired my own space. He told me he did have a smaller area downstairs. The current tenants would be vacating it in a month or so, and that might be more in line with what I needed. We set up an appointment for me to see it the following week. I felt like a kid waiting for a trip to Disney, there were butterflies in my tummy and a sense of anticipation I hadn't had in years!

The day I met with the manager, he told me the smaller room was no longer available. The business occupying the space was not sure about moving and so it was extending its lease month to month until it was ready to leave. He suggested I look at the larger space. Even though I felt it was too big, I agreed to check it out as long as I was there.

The minute I saw the space I felt it could become my new healing center. Why not? Maybe the Universe had bigger plans for me. Maybe it was time to skip a step and move right into the big leagues. I could do this! I could make it work! My mind/ego whirled with possibilities while my gut and higher self were screaming out DON'T DO IT! WAIT. IT'S NOT FOR YOU! Still, the light was perfect and it felt peaceful and calm, like a great big hug. I was so excited! I told him I'd take it.

The landlord gave me a month to fill two more treatment rooms. This way three of the five rooms would be filled and that was the minimum amount of rent he could accept. We could stay like that for a time, but the understanding was to eventually fill all five rooms with working practitioners. I knew a lot of people and figured it would be a snap to do this.

The following week I was to fly to Sedona to take my Karuna Reiki® Master training. I was so excited to receive this attunement and see what this level had in store for me. In retrospect I laugh as I type this because it was the perfect timing for me to heal so many things.

I called two women I knew who were looking for a space and they agreed to contact the landlord and take a look at the place while I was gone. My plan was for all of us to sign leases upon my return. Things seemed to be rolling right along. It was a dream come true.

Well, not exactly I got a call in Sedona telling me the two women did not feel the space fit their needs and declined. I was back to square one. I told the landlord I was confident I could find two others to fill the rooms and I'd work on it when I returned.

Upon my return I put the word out that I needed two office mates. I talked to everyone I knew, including my clients. Two of my clients, students of mine who were Level Two Reiki practitioners, both felt they would like to rent a room.

Here was the first of many mistakes I made. I intuitively felt that they might not be ready. They had recently received their Reiki Level Two and were not yet working on people. They both felt that this was something they could afford and it would motivate them to keep moving forward. I liked them and was caught up in their enthusiasm, but the defining factor for me was they could help me secure the space. I would have the three rooms rented and so the landlord would allow me to stay. I wish I'd listened to my initial intuitive voice and waited. But I was too caught up in the excitement and momentum and moved forward full speed ahead, intuition be damned! It was quite a reckless thing to do, but in retrospect I needed to experience these lessons.

The day we met to sign the lease I woke up with a sense of foreboding. I ignored it and went to the space. The energy was different, heavier, but I continued to ignore these signals. I wanted to make this work. We each signed our own lease and would be responsible for our own rent. As I was signing the lease, my inner voice screamed, "NO! NO! NO!" I signed and smiled. It would be okay, I told myself, even if it didn't feel right.

It was a tumultuous couple of months. Things went downhill pretty quickly after that I'm sad to say. I had just returned from my Karuna Reiki® training and this new energy was coursing through me. In retrospect I see it gave me exactly what I needed to heal some things that were ready to be healed, but I didn't see that at the time.

I made so many mistakes! I wasn't listening to my higher self, allowing myself to be divinely guided. I was forcing my will on things and it wasn't working and it wasn't pretty. Old patterns were emerging and I didn't recognize them. My ego was fully engaged.

A trip to Ikea proved to be the beginning of the end of this co-op experience. I was all jazzed up, hyper, nervous, and crabby that day. I knew I shouldn't go; yet I still did. Driving down the freeway a piece of wood flew off the car in front of me and hit both my car and my suite mates behind me, doing a major amount of damage. Undeterred we continued. I remember standing on the side of the freeway, looking at the crows circling overhead and knowing I should just go home, yet I persevered.

I whirled around Ikea while the two of them looked at everything in slow motion. I was impatient and annoyed. I felt so unsettled, so crazy. I'd just started a routine of bio-identical hormones and this may have added to my distress. I also started a new part-time job the week before and it was freaking me out. I was in over my head. The thought of rent in the cooperative scared me to death. I was going against my intuition and it was manifesting as bad behavior on my part. I was scared. I knew I'd made a mistake and I had hoped it would all work out. My body was telling me otherwise.

Things went from bad to worse. I've never communicated so poorly in my life. I kept trying to make things right. I kept trying to explain myself. Nothing worked. It continued to spiral down and some of my worst fears materialized.

My big fear is being left out, being talked about, not being included. All of this happened. My two partners became close and sort of banded against me. It felt horrible. I dreaded going in to work. *All I wanted to do was do Reiki! Why can't we all just get along?* This is a familiar theme in my life and here it was, being replayed again on a very large level. That newly attuned Karuna energy was doing its job and it was now time to heal.

Of course, at the time I wasn't aware of any of this. Thick in the middle of it, all I felt was pain, frustration, betrayal and confusion. I stayed away, worked at home, hid. I couldn't allow myself to think of any of it. I was on the run. (Which was my M.O. at the time. I ran from conflict or hid behind the "peace and love" façade.)

One morning, I heard a voice telling me to go to the gym, to work it out of my system. I went to a water aerobics class and the instructor, a friend of mine, said something that became a catalyst for change. She asked me how my sister was doing and I replied "she's having a hard time at her job and if she doesn't make some changes she's going to lose it." BINGO! I knew I had to do something; I just wasn't sure what to do. Yet, I knew it was coming. Again it was one of those things I had to trust.

After the class I went home and called my landlord. The words spilled out of my mouth before I even had a chance to think about them. I told him I had made a mistake, I was unhappy with the current space and needed to move. I told him I'd eat the money for the year's lease if I had to. He listened and then told me that the original space I wanted downstairs just became available. The folks that couldn't make up their mind just did. He told me they were leaving in a month and if I could sit tight I could have the space. I thanked him and then jumped around my home in glee!

I called my husband, the stable one in the family, who had custody of the finances. He normally says no to any new venture, partly out of fear, partly out of caution. This time he said, "Do it! It's time! You deserve it." Oh, my!

I signed a new lease for the new space, and moved downstairs the following month. There were two large rooms; one for classes and one that held two tables for treatments. The energy was amazing and I could do what I wanted when I wanted for the first time ever. I furnished it in a fun and funky fashion. My client load had increased as had my classes and I was on the way to doing all of those things I'd always wanted to do.

Yet.

I still had an unsettled feeling. My mental monkey mind worked overtime, filing me with fear, dread and what ifs. Part of it was the guilt and shame that came with my leaving the co-op experience after only a few months. I'm not one to walk away from things unresolved. I like things tied up nice and neat and it was not. It was messy and hurt feelings were still all over the place. Guilt. Shame. They were almost physical entities in my rooms, haunting me. How could something that started out with such good intentions turn out so badly?

I didn't know what to do so I did nothing. Eventually the guilt and shame faded and I thought less about what had happened and focused more on my new burgeoning practice. And my, how it burgeoned! I still worried about running into my partners from upstairs yet I never did. I also was concerned about them trash talking me in the Reiki community. That was probably my biggest fear. I hoped that one day we'd be able to work it out and I could truly see the experience as a blessing and a healing. I never did work things out with them but I am forever grateful for the healing and blessings they gave me.

I learned some big lessons right out of the gate. I will remember these two women as angels who helped pave the way for me to create and sustain my successful Reiki practice. I am forever grateful to them, and also to Karuna Reiki®. I'd been just swimming in that newly attuned energy without realizing it! It brought all my stuff front and center, with me completely unaware.

I think once I admitted I had made a mistake, surrendered, and was willing to do whatever it took, I heard the voice. I followed that voice and it took me to where I should have been originally. However, I learned many things during those short, tumultuous months, things I needed to learn and understand about others and myself. Some of those things:

Trust your gut!

When I heard "the voice" during the time upstairs I ignored it. It scared me to do what it told me. I also had an "agenda" and I kept pushing up stream to make it succeed. It did not.

Speak up!

I am not a shy person, nor am I one to keep quiet about things that are important to me. Yet during this time I held back and let things pile up. I was confused and frustrated and didn't know what to do. Normally when faced with indecision I do nothing. Yet it didn't feel right. I knew what I needed to do, but I was fearful to do it. So I held back and my fear, frustration, and confusion led to anger, which would leak out inappropriately.

It was unprofessional and I am not proud of my behavior. I was like a railroad train roaring down the tracks, not to be stopped. This energy spilled out onto the others and we all mirrored each other's worst behavior. In retrospect I see that had I openly and honestly came from my heart and talked about my feelings, instead of hiding behind my fear or railroading my agenda things might have turned out differently. Maybe not. But I do know you can't lose when you express yourself from your heart.

Don't be afraid to make a mistake (and admit it!)

I've heard many stories from Reiki peers, clients and students who have started and stopped or made mistakes in the beginning of their careers. It's okay. Mistakes are how we learn. Don't be afraid to keep going, and please take the time to listen to your guidance and be honest with yourself and others. There is no place for shame or fear here. We are human. We are learning.

Know that you deserve good! Have faith in your abilities. Stretch yourself. And if you are fearful, Do It Afraid!

That pretty much says it all. I look back at the insecure, scared woman and wonder how I even got as far as I did. What was I so afraid of?

Never do anything for the money!

I could give you a million examples (really!) of things I've done wrong because I was worried about money. It seems for the longest time, I made all of my decisions based on money. I had to learn some hard lessons around this, due to my fear of lack. I know this stems from my family of origin and how I lived for many years as a poor, single woman. I see many of my students starting out struggling with the same issue. I feel for them. I know what that is like. Here's how I finally, once and for all healed that issue.

One Step Forward, Two Steps Back

I had quit my "real world job" and began my Reiki practice. It was a slow start but I was doing well. At about the six-month mark I experienced more cancellations and a lighter workload than the previous months. This spooked me and so I took a part-time job, 20 hours a week. I had many reasons for taking this job but if I'm honest I know that I took it because I didn't feel I could earn enough money practicing Reiki. I still did not consider it a "real job". And as long as I had that thought process that would be true.

It is interesting to note that I had the job interview the same day I met the landlord to look at the larger space. Everything about that day screamed *wrong* but my will was still stronger than my intuition, so I charged ahead on all levels.

So I began work in a job that I wasn't entirely suited for, but it paid well and the hours were good. It was also for a great company and that helped to justify things for me. Still, the job was a bad match but I wasn't allowing myself to acknowledge that. What it did do for me was alleviate my money worries. With this job I could pay my rent, and have extra money. If I had a cancellation or slow week I didn't worry. Instead I enjoyed the extra time and worked on my marketing or teaching materials. It really took the pressure off.

Except . . . My practice started to grow. I had new clients coming out of the woodwork and my classes increased from one a month to three or four per month. I began working every day of the week, with zero days off. I'd work three days at my real job and 4 days at Reiki. I did this for about six months until I realized something had to give; I was running on empty.

One bright winter morning I sat down in my healing center, warm and cozy in the sun. I asked Reiki to guide me in meditation, to help me, to show me the next steps. I employed the distant symbol (HSZSN) and asked that whatever I do it be for the best and highest good of others and myself. Immediately I saw a small white picket fence. I understood the fence represented my resistance. I saw the fence come down and paper money of all denominations flowing over it. The message was clear—if I released my fear of lack, the money would flow.

I had choices. I could quit my job and focus on my Reiki practice, keep going as is, or just work at my other job. I *knew* the answer in my gut, but I still had that fear of "what if?" as in "What if no one comes?" "What if I fail?" "What if I make the wrong choice?"

That night I was guided (the voice once again!) to attend a group meditation. This is not something I would normally do. It was a work night, deep into winter, snowing and about 20 miles from my home. Yet I knew I needed to be there. After the meditation there was a Q&A and one woman stood up and asked about her job. She was a social worker, working in a hospital (for the money) yet yearned to grow her private practice. She couldn't because the hospital took up all of her time. It could have been me speaking, yet at the time I didn't realize it.

In my head, I thought, "Well, duh, quit your hospital job and do what you love!" It seemed simple enough and I couldn't understand what her problem was. The teacher's answer mirrored my thoughts although with more compassion and understanding. It was at that moment that the light bulb went off! "QUIT YOUR JOB"! I went in the next day and gave my notice. I left a month later and my practice exploded.

The Call—My Path to Reiki

It took many, many lessons for me to finally get this. And if there is one single thing that my students want to talk about it is how can they survive "just" doing Reiki. They long to quit their real jobs and follow the Reiki path. I share my story with them, but many are stuck, and like me have to learn the lesson over and over and over, until they come to the point where they are ready to let go and surrender. It's a process and one can tell another but I believe it's all a lesson we have to learn, each in our own way. We all have different financial circumstances, risk and trust levels. We need to test ours.

Many people told me and I read it in several books, but until I had the experience for myself, I didn't trust or believe that I could do it. And I see myself telling so many others, knowing they, too, don't trust or believe it. But I still help to plant those seeds.

Tell the Truth—All of It

When I first wrote about my path to Reiki I kept this section out. I was embarrassed and ashamed and didn't want to go back down that path. Yet, I feel it is important to include these experiences as they illustrate the fear and confusion I went through in this process. I had a hard time starting out, and I made a lot of mistakes. I was emotional and scared and blind at times, to myself and to others. It was part of my journey I now see and I am grateful to be reminded of this and to have the courage to leave it in the book. The finished product-my growing Reiki practice-looked much different in the beginning. I believe these examples can give others hope.

My Successful Practice

Doing Reiki every day and teaching on the weekends helped to continue to bring up my stuff. I ended up leaving the job at the hospital and once again gave all the attention to my Reiki practice. I practiced and taught. A couple of women I knew in the community came in and taught classes and mini-retreats at my healing center. It became a gathering place. Weekends found me teaching Reiki or at one of the mini-retreats learning about Shamanic practices, writing, or meditating. It was exactly what I'd envisioned and it was wonderful!

Soon it would it would be time to renew my lease and I had to decide if I wanted to stay or move on to another space. The landlord was talking about a multiple year lease so I had to make up my mind. While I was happy with the way things were, I really didn't want to stay in that space, as it held too many painful memories. I was also really busy with all of the weekend workshops and was starting to feel that things were getting bigger and busier than I wanted to be. I longed for the days of just doing Reiki and teaching.

I felt once again like a meeting planner, juggling all of the workshops and retreats. I was very grateful for the opportunity, don't get me wrong. But things seemed to be headed in a direction that I didn't want to go. I felt it was time to make a change. In retrospect I see that I was slowly but surely finding my way. I went from the gym, to a clinic where I shared a room to a shared center to my own space. What was next?

Back to the Clinic

I went to Sedona with my husband for his annual birthday vacation that spring. Like so many times before I knew Sedona held some answers for me, so I asked, went and listened, hoping to hear what was next.

I thought I had wanted my own space. While it was a rocky beginning once I moved downstairs I began to fulfill my dream. I brought in other women to teach workshops and they were well attended. I began a monthly Reiki Share for my students, a sort of continuing education get together. Most months as many as twelve women would be there, working at 3 tables. It was inspiring, educational and fun.

So why was I restless? What was I looking for? Why did I want to leave? Because it just did not feel right. The business upstairs still haunted me, but it was more than that. There was an energy in the space that just did not feel good. I hired a Feng Shui consultant to help me out and she felt it as well. She said to me, "*This place is good for money but bad for people.*" So far that proved to be true. I was very busy and making a decent wage, but there seemed to be an unusual amount of negative energy from clients and other tenants in the building. The consultant went on to tell me that I needn't worry, as I would be moving soon.

But where would I go? I remember thinking, "I wish I could go back to the acupuncture clinic, but with my own room." As much as I wanted to return, I knew I needed my own space. I didn't see how that was possible with the limited number of rooms.

The consultant proved to be right. A day after I had that thought about moving back to the clinic, with my own room (while in Sedona!) I received a call from the clinic owner. She told me she was thinking about knocking down some walls and building out her space. She was going to add three more rooms and was looking for a couple of practitioners. Each of us would have our own room and the rent was very fair. Oh, my God! Just what I'd been wishing for! I told her I would come by when I returned from vacation to discuss it further.

When I got back into town we met and she showed me the plans. The room she wanted me to take was not exactly what I had in mind so I was slow to commit. I worried there would be a lot of noise as it was next to the kitchen. I have a real thing with noise when I am practicing. I had to go out of town for a conference and I told her I'd let her know when I returned the following Monday.

All weekend at the conference I was distracted. My monkey mind whirled! Back and forth it went, weighing the pros and cons. By the time I was in the airport ready to head back on Sunday night I was leaning towards not taking the space. I would work something else out. It turned out the Universe had other plans for me, and was there to save me from myself.

My flight was delayed due to severe weather in the Midwest. While waiting my husband called and said he had some bad news. He had gotten a call from my landlord that morning telling him that my center had flooded and the floor was covered with about six inches of standing water. The carpets were ruined, and the water had risen to partly cover the furniture.

He and the landlord worked all day to clean things up. When I went there the next morning it smelled damp and musty. Giant fans were blowing, trying to dry things out. It was determined that my office would be out of commission for at least a week.

This was not the news I wanted to hear as I had a busy, full week of clients. I called the clinic owner and asked her if I could temporarily use a room for the week. I told her I still hadn't made up my mind. She very graciously offered me the room free of charge for as long as I needed it and suggested it might be a "trial run." I agreed and worked there for a week.

It didn't take more than a day working back in this wonderful energy for me to realize it was where I belonged. I was back home. I hadn't realized how much I missed that place, where I was back among like-minded folks. My year and a half away was a time of big lessons for me and while it had been extremely difficult, and at times seemingly impossible, I learned so much and I am so grateful for it. What felt like failure actually turned out to be growth and progress on many levels. When we are in that place, we cannot see the positive aspects, but with some space and time, I now see it was exactly what I needed. I'm glad I persevered and kept moving forward.

Possibly for the first time in my life, I felt the confidence of standing in my own power, I learned that not everyone is going to like me or what I have to say, and that it is okay. My self-worth is not dependent on others. I learned how to listen to my guides, even when my mind would tell me otherwise. I learned how to take what I learned in the corporate world and apply it to my new business. I learned how to put my stamp on it, do it my way and be okay with that. I learned how to Do It Afraid.

Much of this time, I was terrified. I felt like I was flying by the seat of my pants. It was the first time in my working life that I didn't have a template; I wasn't being told what to do; I was having to forge ahead, trusting my gut and my guides. I remembered hearing something in a class years before about going out into the snow, with no path and just making your own. No worries about where you are going, rather creating your own imprint in the snow. I was doing that. That image delighted me and gave me courage and when I'd falter or think about chucking it all because it was too hard I'd conjure up that image and keep moving forward.

I worked in that clinic for four more years, until I moved to Arizona. It proved to be a good decision. I had co-workers that were professional and respectful of each other. I worked in a beautiful, nurturing space, in a good location that was safe. I used to ask for all of these things in an affirmation while I drove to work years earlier, when things weren't going so well. I manifested it!

Enough about me. Let's now discuss how you are going to create and sustain *your* Reiki practice.

QUESTIONS TO PONDER
CHECKLIST

☐ Has Reiki called you? Can you allow yourself to heed the call?

☐ Do you recognize your intuition? Are you able to discern how you receive it?

☐ Have you had a Reiki session? If not, go get one. If so, how often? I like to say if you have the time and the money, get a session every 4 to 6 weeks to keep yourself in balance.

☐ Have you taken a class? If not, consider an "Intro to Reiki" or a Level One class. If so, consider going to the next level.

☐ If you are already a Reiki Master, give yourself permission to think (just a little) about how and where you'd like to practice. Fantasize! Start the process!

SECTION TWO

Do It Afraid

Getting Ready

I n this chapter, I'd like to share some thoughts on Reiki and getting ready to start your practice. You may have had some of these thoughts or feelings. You may have had similar experiences. It helped me to know that I was not alone, that my fears and insecurities were more common than I realized. This stuff is not so readily discussed so I'd like to put it out there. After reading, examine how you feel about all of this. How do you feel about Reiki, starting a practice, being a Reiki Master? Let's plant the seeds that will become your practice. You are on your way!

Practice, Practice, Practice

First and foremost, practice! They don't call it practice for nothing. The one thing I know for sure about Reiki is that you have to do it to know it. You can read books, take classes and talk about it until you are blue in the face but the only way you are going to get to know it is by doing it. There are no shortcuts.

Practice every day on yourself. So many people tell me "I don't have time!" or "I don't have anyone to work on." Sure you do. Work on yourself! I tell them to put their hands on themselves when they lie down to go to sleep. You're lying there anyways; you might as well give yourself Reiki. Do the same thing when you wake up in the morning; give yourself some Reiki to begin your day. This is the very least you can do.

I know a man who has a stressful job in a big corporation. He goes into the bathroom when he feels stressed and gives himself

Reiki. I used to put my hands on my legs, not visible under the conference table, and give myself Reiki in meetings. In my car at stop signs I give myself Reiki. Stuck in traffic I give myself Reiki. You get the picture. Find creative ways to give yourself Reiki. It's a gift to yourself. You deserve it.

And remember, the more Reiki you do the stronger your channel becomes. You can also send distant Reiki to your loved ones, the earth, everyone and anything. Do it! Don't make excuses. You are developing your relationship with Reiki. You are getting ready. Make it your daily practice.

Find Your Path

Reiki was my ticket to the light. What is yours? There are many paths up the mountain. Everyone is healing from something. Everyone can be healed by something. Once you find your path how do you make it work? In the beginning there were so many things I wanted to study. All at once! Reiki! Meditation! Shamanism! Breathwork! Writing!

I was all over the place, like a kid in a candy store. So many new ideas and modalities were presenting themselves to me and I had a hard time focusing. For a while I just indulged in all of it and in time the focus narrowed and I zoomed in on Reiki. It called me and I listened. All of those other modalities have become tools that help to enhance my Reiki practice, with Reiki being the main focus. What is calling you? Ask and listen for the answer.

Do What You Need to Do

When I quit the corporate world to go into my practice I did have some money concerns but not enough to stop me. Although there were many people who thought I was crazy, it never really occurred to me it wouldn't work. I went into it assuming I would succeed. I didn't know at the time that many Reiki Masters were not able to make a living doing Reiki and teaching. I assumed I could and I went with that. I figured if I prepared and studied and worked hard I would succeed. And because I believed that I did. It was my reality.

How did I do this? I share below what I did both to inspire you and to help you find ways of your own.

☐ The biggest thing and something that will be repeated through-out this book is I used Reiki to help me move forward. I employed the symbols daily as part of my morning practice. Reiki is the gift that keeps us giving. It calms us down, gives us strength, and clears the path for us, allowing us to move forward. It's such a simple thing. Use it!

☐ I read pretty much everything I could get my hands on regard-ing not only Reiki but self-discovery. This really helped me. I knew I had a lot of healing to do to get over my fears and insecurities that had previously kept me stuck in wanting but not doing. Louise Hay's *You Can Heal Your Life* and Don Miquel Ruiz's *The Four Agreements* were my two favorites. I highly recommend them.

☐ I started venturing out of my comfort zone and began attending classes to expand not only my knowledge but also my circle of acquaintances. I wanted to align myself with like-minded people and learn new ways of thinking and being.

☐ I took meditation classes and learned how to meditate. I found a great teacher who appealed to my Virgo side. The first half of the class we received handouts and she talked about medita-tion. The second half of the class we meditated. I did this for about a year until I was comfortable doing it on my own. Then I began a daily practice. Meditation keeps me sane and grounded.

☐ I began to write. And write. And write. I found a book that had excellent prompts and I would sit on my porch each evening and write my brains out. It was an excellent release and it's my way of discovering things about myself. Find *your* way and do it. Do something to help you to let go of your fears and insecurities and find your way forward.

These are just a few things, but the bigger things I did to help me acclimate to this new way of living and working. They helped me navigate the shifting waters of my life. I had no role models at that time, nor did I know anyone personally who had gone through this sort of shift. Again, and I can't stress it enough, find *your* way. What will help *you* feel comfortable entering this new life, this strange and scary new land? Ask yourself, ask Reiki, listen, trust and take action.

Easy for me to say now, from this vantage point. I had to figure it out and I did. But that's not to say there weren't times I worried. There were. But those times were steeped in ego and fear and it was Reiki's way of teaching me something, to heal that particular fear. The reality was my husband made a good living so even if I failed I would be okay.

At least that is what everyone told me! If I had a dollar for every time someone said to me "Well, you have your husband to lean on, so you don't have to worry," or something similar I'd be rich and never would have had to start a business. I could just collect money from all of the naysayers!

Here's the thing they didn't understand-I would have done it anyway. It was just burning too brightly inside of me. I would have found a way. And yes, even though I had my husband's income to help me out I never really thought about it. Instead I focused on what I needed and how to go about doing it. I kept moving forward.

When I was 25, I was single, living alone, working full-time and going to college part-time. I had a busy life and lived check to check, with no real bank account. I had an opportunity to take a vacation free of charge. An old boyfriend was going to the Grand Canyon and Death Valley for two weeks and his travelling companion dropped out at the last minute. He asked me if I could take his friend's spot, all expenses paid. I told him, "*Yes! Of course!*"

My boss denied my request for two weeks off so I quit my job. She, and pretty much everyone I knew told me I was nuts, and wondered what I was going to do, how I was going to pay my rent, eat, live. I can't explain it other than to say I was guided and I trusted it would all work out and be okay. And it did.

I had a glorious two weeks camping with an ex that turned into a dear friend, climbed into and out of the Grand Canyon, and slept under the stars in just a sleeping bag. It was magnificent and to this day probably one of the better vacations of my life (and I've had a lot of good vacations). We got home on a Sunday and on Monday I went to Manpower and secured a temp position, which turned into a permanent job within a few months.

Moral of this story—don't be afraid to take a risk. Jump! Trust that you will be guided and supported. Once you do this you will discover just how much of you holding yourself back was fear, ego and insecurities.

See Yourself Prosperous

I knew a few Reiki Masters when I started who were struggling, but I figured it meant they weren't trying hard enough, weren't organized enough, or just didn't know business. I know so many excellent Reiki Masters who don't know a lick about business so their practice is always wanting. Many work second and third jobs to make ends meet. This is their reality but it wasn't going to be mine. And it doesn't have to be yours.

I met my current teacher about five years into my Reiki career. She is a successful role model. She is one of the hardest working

Reiki people I know and she has a thriving Reiki practice. I used her for inspiration and modeled many of my business practices after her. This really gave my business a boost. I believe you get what you put into it.

Reiki is hard work, just like any other job. This surprised me but it shouldn't have. While Reiki is as simple as putting your hands on the person and getting out of the way, creating a Reiki Practice is much, much more. The beauty is that you can use Reiki to help grow your business. Win/win! You get what you put into it and what you believe. Mind your thoughts!

Yes, affirmations work. Trust works. Vision Boards work. But *you have to work.* Do it all. And remember to discover and use your gifts, tools and experiences. Put it all towards your practice and it *will* thrive.

Do Your Work

Do your inner work! This type of work requires it. You can't hide. I've been on this path for 15 years and all of those years have been spent in some form of self-discovery. Reiki was the giant key that opened that door for me. I use Reiki and through Reiki I've discovered other teachers that have helped me unpeel the layers of ego and fear I've kept myself shrouded in. It is a big process and not for the faint of heart. Tools that work for me have been Reiki, therapeutic and shamanic breathwork, shamanic journeying, talk therapy, bodywork, reading and writing. Find what works for you, as there are many paths up the mountain.

And while this work has been liberating it has also been terrifying. I met a lot of my boogeymen along the way. I remembered things I'd rather not have. I discovered sides of myself and was horrified and shamed and scared and wanted to quit a million times. Sometimes I did and then humbled myself and went back.

Getting Ready

The bottom line is I did my work (and continue to do so). Most people on this path have to sooner or later. I think it's what separates the wanna-bes from the real thing.

How did I do this? I personally believe I really wanted to heal, so I listened to the guidance and then acted on it. Many times I did not want to. I prefer the magic wand approach, but that's not going to happen. You must pay your dues! (And trust me, it's worth it.) And here's another little nugget-it never ends. Not really. We just keep on evolving.

Ask Yourself Why You Are Doing This

What does success mean to you? Is it money? Fame? Satisfaction in your daily life?

If you are in it for the money this may not be the career for you. It's not that you can't make money, you can. I believe it's more of an attitude, an intention, which I believe is important in doing this type of work.

In Reiki, intention is everything! I've trained many students and I can almost always tell who will be successful and who will not. Those that don't do so well ask me such questions as: How much money can I make? How many clients are you able to see in one day? How much do you charge? I'm going to charge more! You don't charge enough!

So sit down and meditate on why you want to do this. Do you really want this to be your job? Do you feel you are called to it? Or is your ego engaged? Do you want to be seen as a Reiki Master? Is it about the money? Do you truly want to help others heal? What is your motivation? Are you willing to do the work; to do what it takes? Be honest.

Ask Reiki to help you. Better to know these answers going in than to find them out later on. Reiki has a way of bringing our issues front and center. Nip it in the bud and save yourself the trouble if it's not for your best and highest good. While I didn't exactly know the why of doing it, I sure did hear the call and knew that it was something I was supposed to do. It kept after me; I couldn't shake it! Find your truth and then go out and live it.

Fear and Excuses

I was talking to someone the other day in a Reiki class I took. She has a successful job in the corporate world. She works 50 hours a week, travels, and makes a lot of money. She was talking about how much she wished she could do Reiki. I suggested she could keep her job and a few times a month start seeing clients. Or volunteer once a month at a place near her home. At the very least, start attending Reiki Shares to get in the flow and meet other like-minded folks in her community.

With every suggestion she had a reason why she couldn't do it. Most of her reasons centered around time and money. I hear this from so many people that have a desire to start a Reiki practice. I had the same concerns. For me I made the leap when the desire to practice Reiki became stronger than the desire to work in the corporate world. It really was that simple. One day I just knew it was time, after fantasizing about it for years.

I think for a long time I didn't believe I could or would. I kept collecting tools, searching, reading, taking classes, and meeting others with similar goals. I was laying the foundation, getting ready. The fantasizing was like a vision board of my life. I was letting the Universe know I was getting ready. And then I was ready. Once I was there I had to act. So do what you need to do to get ready, but once you are, you have to act.

If you are on the fence and afraid to let go of your job, at least start laying the foundation. Take some classes. Go to Reiki Shares.

Volunteer. Get on a Reiki message board or read a blog. Visualize. Create a vision board. Get into the energy of Reiki. Ask Reiki. Tell the Universe you are ready. Do something. It will come, but not if you are hiding from it. Get it out there!

Fear and Insecurity

I still go through bouts of fear and insecurity. I consider this an occupational hazard, as Reiki tends to bring up our stuff. A few months ago I had a lot of cancellations at the cancer center where I worked, along with changes being made to the program, *and* my classes were not filling up. When I don't work, I don't get paid. Now you would think after all this time I'd be used to the peaks and valleys. Most of the time I am, but this last bout of changes at the center and cancellations proved to be too much. I updated my resume, applied for a job, and a week later I got a bite and an interview.

I dragged out my big leather purse, got dressed up and went to the interview. It felt so good to be out and about in my professional attire. I felt important and enjoyed the ego boost the interview gave me. As I was walking back to my car afterwards, knowing that it went well and that I might be called back for a second interview and possibly offered the job I had a huge "aha" moment. I really didn't want the job. I wanted the attention, I wanted to feel important, and I wanted to be needed. I wanted the income. All of these are ego and fear centered things and if I'm honest I admit to doing this every few years. It can be very hard to sustain a successful Reiki practice.

I have been burned out, with too many clients, and I have been fearful with not enough clients. Most of the time I have balance, but every so often things seem to be out of whack. This is usually when

I am out of control or I need to learn something, instead of just going with the flow and accepting those things I cannot control.

Thus the interview. Luckily I was not the chosen candidate for the position. If I had been I would have declined it. The lesson that came from this was to admit to myself that I was feeling insecure and scared, and, to see how I could heal that. I liked the feeling the whole experience gave me and so I decided to replicate that in my business. I can be honest with my co-workers when I am feeling neglected or not liking the changes. I didn't speak up when these changes occurred; rather I lost my voice and kept my frustration and anger inside. That's old behavior and I can no longer afford to do that.

Not long after the interview I had an opportunity to travel to teach a Holy Fire Reiki class, something I had been recently trained in. I was afraid to go, but I went afraid. I sensed something big was waiting for me. I was right. The very first day of the class in the morning meditation I had a vision of quitting my job at the cancer center, and traveling to teach.

After some fear and worry, I gave my notice at the center, and in the ensuing weeks a number of classes popped up. Imagine that! While I will miss my patients I am grateful to have had the opportunity to create the program and it will continue, giving other Reiki Masters the opportunity to work with this population. I will move forward in my Reiki career, teaching, beefing up my private practice and writing. Reiki allows us to always evolve if we allow ourselves to be in the flow. Pay attention!

Take Care of Yourself
We have to take care of ourselves when we have our own business. Sometimes we get lost. I am learning to pay attention to those feelings when I am out of control. It usually means it is time for a

shift to occur. The interview was a signal I was out of control. I recognized this and asked Reiki for some help. The answer came to me in the meditation and I made the necessary changes. That feeling I had after the interview that I wanted to replicate in my practice? I have it now. And, I dress up more, as I like how that makes me feel.

I focus a lot on the client and the business side of things but I tend to overlook me, and my mental and emotional health. I need to pay better attention to that. I need to ask Reiki to help me. I know this but seem to need to be reminded of it every so often. I see so many Reiki people doing this. Remember yourself. Be honest. Do what you need to do. Don't stay safe. Grow, evolve, and keep moving forward. Even if you are afraid. Especially then. Your soul is speaking to you!

There have been times that I was lean financially or freaked out about cancellations and then I look back and see that everything always balances out. I am always taken care of. I know this on an intellectual level but seem to have forgotten it. Good reminder.

How do you take care of yourself? What are things you can do? Reiki? Massage? Meditation? Classes? Nature? Alone time? Figure out what you need and give yourself not only the time, but also the permission.

Reiki is So Healing

Doing Reiki for a living is the best job I've ever had. I joke that it is the only job you'll have where you want to work when you feel sick. And it's true. No only will Reiki heal you of your mental and emotional challenges, but if you are sick it helps you to feel better. Instead of calling in sick I can't wait to get to work, knowing I'll feel better. And on all levels: mentally, physically, emotionally and spiritually. There have been a few days where I went in to work with a stomachache or headache only to realize halfway through the day that they disappeared. Giving Reiki took it away. Remember, when we give Reiki we get Reiki.

A really good example of this is when my sister-in-law died. She was killed by a hit and run drunk driver. Her death devastated our family. My brother stayed with me for a few days after the accident and so I cancelled all of my Reiki appointments. We were all zombies, in shock over her senseless death. I finally had to go back to work and honestly I just dreaded it. I was heartbroken and sick to my stomach, worried about my brother and still in shock. I had no idea how I was going to be able to work.

I guess I forgot how healing Reiki is. At some point during that first day back I realized I was feeling joy. Not just better, but joy! I know this is hard to believe, but the Reiki flowing through me was so loving and healing and it felt so great. It was the first time I truly experienced how profoundly healing Reiki is. The contrast between how I felt when I came in and how I felt when I went home was remarkable. It took a long time before I felt good all of the time again, but it helped to have the Reiki to go to during the day, to help me with my healing. Don't forget this powerful healing tool. Use it every day, in every way. There are so many possibilities.

Listen—Reiki Whispers

When I began practicing Reiki professionally I started paying attention during sessions at a deeper level. I remember working on a client very early in my career and I kept hearing "stop, stop, stop."

After the session, we were talking and the client told me that at one point in the session her feelings became very intense and she was screaming inside for them to stop. I did not stop when I heard this, as it never occurred to me I might be picking up on something from the client.

This first "hearing" allowed me to really begin paying attention and it changed my sessions. I plugged in at a deeper level and began to trust my intuition. Think of ways you perceive spirit. Do you hear? Know? Feel? Spend some time getting to know this side of yourself, especially when giving a Reiki session. This will help you to plug in deeper as a practitioner, to get into that flow.

Leave Your Friends and Family Alone

When I first read Louise Hay's book, *You Can Heal Your Life*, one piece of advice really stood out: Leave your friends and family alone! I didn't really understand this and certainly didn't think it applied to me so I had to learn this lesson the hard way. Pay attention so you don't have to.

Don't expect your family and friends to support your practice. It's great if they do (and they might) but let go of that expectation. Please don't take it personally if they don't want to have a session or take a class. This isn't about you! If they are guided, great, otherwise leave them alone. Do not expect them to have your same values or adapt to your new way of thinking/being. They are on their own path. Respect that and let them *be*.

Your friends and family are not your clients *and* your clients are not your friends. Got that? This was such a grey area for me in the beginning of my practice.

Clients would want to go to lunch or out for breakfast, or for tea. In the beginning I would do this. This took a large chunk of my time and I became resentful. I was just too afraid to say no. I thought that if I said no they wouldn't like me, get mad, and not come back. That has rarely been the case.

I believe they were confusing the Reiki energy with me. I have done this as well. We feel so good when we get a session that we sometimes feel it is the person giving the session that makes us feel this way, instead of the Reiki. Not true! It's the Reiki! Always! Reiki flows through us and not from us. We are channels. Do not forget this.

Sometimes a client would say, "You are amazing!" or "You are so good at what you do." Big ego check here. You are not responsible for their healing. I would say, "That's the Reiki!" Because they feel so good, they want to stay with that feeling, by being your friend and hanging out with you. I understand. I did the same thing with my teacher.

Be yourself, know it's the Reiki, and learn to say no. What areas of your life can you apply this to? Do you confuse the Reiki energy with the person? Do you have expectations of your friends and family? Take a good look at these areas in your life.

There is Always a Healing Opportunity

If you are doing Reiki every day and teaching it every weekend like I was, your stuff is bound to come up. It appears in the form of clients, students, teachers, peers and co-workers. They are all highly polished mirrors, reflecting back to us what we need to heal. Allow it. Instead of blaming and judging others, ask yourself what you have to learn from each encounter. They are all healing opportunities.

In the beginning I didn't yet know this. I was so emotional and didn't like to sit with the feelings. Reiki is patient and gentle, but it is persistent. It knows what we need even when we don't. Especially when we don't. It will keep whispering in your ear until you hear it and allow it to help you to heal. Be aware. Don't resist, but rather welcome the healing. You will be glad you did.

Getting Ready

Pay Attention to Your Guidance

Pay attention to *how* you receive your guidance. Yesterday I was with a Reiki colleague. She spent most of the day talking about how she looked for "signs," and yearned to *hear* her guides. The rest of the time she spent talking about how she *knew* certain things and based her decisions on them. She recently quit her job and made a big cross-country move, and now she was waiting for guidance. She was getting guidance, even though it did not look like she wanted it to.

I felt badly at one point in our conversation because she kept asking me what I would do if I were in her shoes. I told her I couldn't possibly know. I shared with her that I thought she was incredibly gifted, that she *knew* things and perhaps she should pay attention to that.

If you can, try to recognize the way *you* receive information from your guides. Not everyone hears. There are many different ways to access this information and we all do it differently.

I asked my colleague to pay attention and be grateful for the *knowing* she has. It is a gift and it has served her well. She then asked how I *knew* it was the truth, her guides, not something she is making up? I told her she has to trust.

Bottom line, be quiet and listen. Trust. Those thoughts inside your head just might be the angels or the Reiki guides whispering in your ears. How do you know you are not making it up? For me, it's because I wouldn't make that up, I'd make something else up. My guidance almost never sounds like my mind. Many times, it's just the opposite.

A month or so later I was having a similar conversation with this same woman. She was again frustrated, telling me that every-one tells her to listen. I had the sense that she might have been waiting for or expecting some sort of AHA! type of voice, like maybe

Jesus booming into her ear, so I said, "Well, what do your thoughts tell you? My guidance sounds just like my own voice, my thoughts in my head. The difficult thing for me is to discern which is my guidance and which is me."

B I N G O! She got it. In fact, she shared something she always says and I thought it was brilliant, "It's either Ego or my Higher Self." Yes! Yes! Yes! That led to a very excited discussion where she discovered she actually *has* been hearing guidance all along, it just didn't sound like she thought it would. Wow! I love it when that happens!

Ok, it's time. All of this talking and longing is really you getting ready, putting it out there. In the following chapters I'll share information with you about your practice, from the business side, to clients, classes and teaching. Bon Voyage!

QUESTIONS TO PONDER
CHECKLIST

☐ Are you ready? How does this question make you feel? Are you afraid? Are you ready and willing to Do It Afraid? Meditate on this.

☐ What steps have you taken so far, if any? What steps do you need to take? Can you start with a list?

☐ Are you willing to do the work, both inner and outer? How will you do this?

☐ What tools might you use to assist you in your healing? Books? Writing? Classes? Sessions? Which modalities speak to you? Look into what is available in your community and start moving forward.

☐ Do you practice self-Reiki? Commit to a daily practice

☐ Ask yourself why you want to start a practice. What is your motivation?

☐ Are you able to recognize your fear? In what ways does it manifest?

☐ Create a plan of self-care for yourself.

☐ Pay attention to your inner voice. Listen and take guided action.

Your Reiki Practice

What makes me an authority on creating a Reiki practice? What do I know? I know what worked for me and that is what I share here. Ask yourself what makes *you* an authority on creating your Reiki practice. What do you bring to the table? What experience do you have that you can use to create your own thriving practice? Think of it as another job. That's what I did and it made the whole idea of my practice less intimidating. As I share my story of creating my practice check in to see if any of it resonates with you.

Think of It as Just Another Job

Before I began my practice I spent my career in the corporate world, in medical, airline and academic environments. The last 15 years of my career were spent in jobs that were newly created; meaning prior to my being in the job it didn't exist.

Establishing these new positions provided a challenge for me and allowed me to exercise my creativity. (Which, I believe, gave me the courage to eventually start my practice.) The first position I took was at a big university. My job description was to provide administrative support to the Chairmen of the Journalism and Advertising and Public Relations departments. Easy enough. I took the job because I had recently gotten married and bought a home and I wanted to lighten my workload so I could focus on my new home life. It didn't hurt that it was a nine-month position with summers off.

When I arrived for my interview it was held in one of the Chairmen's offices. Next to his office was a large, empty room. That room would become my office. I would go on to not only furnish the room with everything from window dressings and furniture but also phones, computers and student workers. When I left years later it would be a thriving, fully functioning office.

It seemed like a large order upon accepting the job and not one I might have applied for had I known all of the parameters of the position, but once there I discovered I had a knack for creating something out of nothing. How did I do this? I just kept doing the next thing that was needed to make it work. While I am able to see things on a big picture level, when creating something new I'm better at knowing the desired outcome while focusing on the task at hand, one step at a time until I achieve my goal.

My next couple of positions were similar. I'd come into a job that didn't previously exist and I'd make it work. These positions became increasingly more difficult with greater responsibility and I discovered I loved a challenge.

I see my Reiki practice as one more job that didn't exist before I stepped into it. I have once again created something out of nothing. I came equipped with knowledge and experience, saw the big picture, had a goal (a thriving Reiki practice) and just kept doing the next thing needed to make it work. Don't overwhelm yourself with the big picture. Know what it is but break it into manageable steps, one at a time. You *will* get there.

Keep Moving Forward, Despite the Obstacles

Before I talk about starting your practice, I'd like to share a question I just got from one of my students. She was getting ready to spread her wings and start her practice. Because she was feeling scared and unsure of herself and her decision to start a practice she decided to share her thoughts and feelings with her family. Their response only made her more unsure and scared. If this happens to you know this is par for the course.

These questions come up all the time and I think you'll be able to relate. You've probably experienced some variety of what's written below by well meaning friends or family and it can be enough to derail your plans. Don't let it. Acknowledge their advice, thank them, know what is in your heart and discern what is best for you. And remember, if you are afraid, Do It Afraid.

What Do You Do When Your Family Won't Support Your Goals and Dreams?

"... I feel attacked by them! They all think they know what's best for me!"

Just last night, I had a student call and say those words to me. It made me grateful I was writing this book so others can read these words and know they are not alone.

I can relate. I didn't get a whole lot of support from my family and friends when I started, yet I expected it. So I guess you could say I set myself up for disappointment. I did get a lot of comments and advice, most of it unasked for, yet people thought I needed to know these things. Off the top of my head here are some comments I can remember, all of them hurtful and crazy-making to me.

- ❐ Are you insane?
- ❐ What are you going to do for money?
- ❐ What about insurance?
- ❐ Will your husband let you do this?
- ❐ Why do you have to quit your job?
- ❐ Is this a mid-life crisis?
- ❐ You re-invent yourself every so often, don't you?

That's all I can remember and it's enough. At the time I really let these comments get to me. I was already on shaky ground. I wasn't yet used to listening to my guidance and that's all I had to go on. I knew that I needed to make these changes in my life and go down this path of Reiki. I wasn't sure why, but I trusted the voice. I found it hard to tell people this and honestly I wondered why I even had to. I didn't need to engage or let it get to me, yet I did. It was exhausting but I didn't let it change my mind. However, it did add fuel to the fear. Still, I kept going.

My advice to you is despite the best attempts of your loved ones to derail you, is to keep moving forward. They love you and want what's best for you. They don't understand and their advice is based on their experiences and their fear. It's not yours. You don't have to engage. Thank them and walk away. End of conversation. You can do it and you will be glad you did. Is it easy? No. But it is easier than debating your choices. Be true to yourself and go after your dreams. You can do it.

Use Your Fear To Motivate You

I spoke with a client recently about starting her practice. She has an opportunity to rent a space, a really great space, with another practitioner. She has been a Reiki Master for almost ten years and for the last five or so has wanted to start her practice. She has been doing a lot of freebies, working on friends and family, but feels it is time to hang out her shingle. She is terrified to take this step. She had a lot of reasons why it might not work, but one reason why it might. She is ready.

I recognize those feelings. I felt that way when I started at the spa, when I went into the community and when I moved into my own space. These were all firsts, and they were fraught with fear and insecurity. Remember Reiki brings up our stuff and this can help us move to the next level of our healing. Use the fear to your advantage; let it motivate you. Please know that everyone is afraid and has doubts. Transcend this and Do It Afraid. My fear never matched the reality of the situation. It was just fear. Know that and know you are not alone in these feelings. We all experience this.

Be Who You Are

I know a woman who just moved to a new city. She has been meeting her new neighbors and they have been asking her what she does for a living. It is her intention to leave the corporate world behind and begin a Reiki practice in her new town.

Yet she is afraid to tell them the truth. She wondered if they won't like her or if her being a Reiki Master will offend them. I understand this fear. I've been there.

When I started practicing Reiki I worked at a Catholic Women's College. Many of my colleagues and one of my bosses was a nun. I was fearful of talking about Reiki to them so I didn't. I kept it a secret. When I was leaving to grow my business one of the Sisters asked me what my business was and I had to come clean. She said "What? You do Reiki?"

I was a shivering wreck, afraid to answer, when she said, "I wish you had told me, as I've been going to someone else. I would love to come to you!" Wow! That was not the reaction I'd expected. My fear of revealing what I did (and my true self) kept me from working with her and probably many others. Not long after this conversation I began teaching at this college, and a few of the nuns took my classes and came to me for Reiki sessions.

Don't be afraid to tell people who you are and what you do. Respect Reiki. Respect yourself.

Your Reiki Practice

Where Should You Practice? Considering Space

So how do you go about getting started? First things first, you need a place to practice. Where will that be? You have some options. You can work from your home, have table will travel or rent a space.

Working From Home

You need to consider your financial situation and work style to know what will work best for you. The most economical way to do this is to work from home. You'll need an extra room, a Reiki/massage table and whatever else you wish to put in the room to make it comfortable and appealing to your clients.

I believe it is important to have a dedicated space for your Reiki room, a sacred space to allow for privacy and comfort. I used to go to a Reiki Master who'd put her table up in the middle of her living room and I didn't like how that felt. I could see her laundry basket and her dirty dishes in the sink. It seemed like an afterthought, as if not enough attention or respect was given to the Reiki.

And while she was an amazing practitioner, probably the best I'd ever gone to, I never felt comfortable in the space. I think it's so important for the client to be comfortable and relaxed, so they may fully give themselves to the Reiki. Minimize the distractions!

Have Table Will Travel

If you are not comfortable with bringing clients into your home and still want an economical option you might want to consider making house calls. I did this when I first learned Reiki, before I began my business. I didn't yet have a dedicated space and I was nervous about bringing people into my home, so I bought a lightweight portable table and went to my client's homes. It was a lot of work and you really can't control your environment, but it worked for a while. People loved me coming to their home. It was easy for them and they were very comfortable in their own environment. I'd bring my boom box and Reiki music and sometimes a candle if they were ok with that.

Renting a Space

If you want to rent a space outside of your home you have many choices. You can rent a singular space just for yourself. You can sublease space with one or more practitioners where you share a room or have one of your own. You can be an employee of a spa, gym, hair salon, or other type of existing business, or you can be a contracted employee in a hospital or hospice. I'm sure there are more choices, but these are the ones I've done and am familiar with.

Ask Yourself How You Like to Work

☐   Do you like being a part of a team?

☐   Are you a loner?

☐   Do you want to be the boss?

☐   How are you at taking direction?

☐   Are you comfortable sharing a room, or a space?

☐   How does your personality lend to each of these types of scenarios?

☐   What is your budget?

☐   Do you have furniture to fill a space? A room?

I never really thought about any of this before I started. I knew I wanted to practice but I didn't think too much about what that would look like. If I thought too hard in those early days I'd run away in fear. So I was practicing my Do It Afraid mantra and just kept putting one foot in front of the other and listening for that guidance. It always came but I didn't always follow it. That's another story.

Employee of an Existing Space

My first Reiki job (after working at home and "have table, will travel") was part of a spa environment, where I was an employee of a gym. I played by their rules and received a paycheck. I had a built in audience (members of the gym) and learned many useful skills. It was the perfect way to begin my career. As a condition of my employment I had to give community talks about "What is Reiki" and do "Reiki Samplers". This got me out of myself and helped me to heal and face many of my fears. I was indeed Doing It Afraid. It was a good first gig.

If you are just starting out you might want to consider doing something like this, being part of an already established business. You have virtually no overhead. The gym provided the room, the table and all of the furnishings. It had a boom box and I would bring in my music and candles. I also brought some crystals to add some energy to the room. Another thing I did was place a bowl of polished stones in the room and every time I had a new client I would give them a stone. I'd tell them this was their "Reiki rock" and when they wanted to get back that feeling of having been on the table they could hold the stone. People loved this! I like giving and who doesn't like receiving?

I also brought in some aromatherapy and would spray the room with lavender essential oil. Be careful with this, though, as not everyone is a fan of scents, and some are even allergic. Regarding pay: I started with a 60/40 split (them 60, me 40) and after a few months, the split became 50/50.

Since I was new at this and had no private clients I felt it was fair. After all, I wasn't paying rent; there was no overhead. The best feature of all of this type of employment was the built in audience. They provided the clients and the marketing. I think this is the best possible job for a beginning Reiki practitioner.

Sharing a Room in a Larger Clinic

After I was at the gym for a year, I wanted to branch out into the community. I decided to look for another established business, as I still wasn't sure how committed I was to this new idea of being a Reiki practitioner. Even though I had just quit my part-time job and was going to try to make a go of it, I still wanted to feel some sort of security and I didn't want to make a huge investment.

I became part of a team at an established acupuncture clinic. The nice thing about moving to this space was the woman I rented from only charged me per client. I paid her $15 every time I saw a client. I kept a list and at the end of the month I paid her. She capped the monthly fee at $400. That first month, my rent was $60 as I only saw four clients. This was an excellent way to start, as there was no pressure to meet my rent.

I had to share the space with three other practitioners and it worked out well as we were all part-time. The three of us shared two rooms. While this worked well financially I soon discovered that I didn't like not knowing what room I'd be in or physically sharing the space as energetically it sometimes felt off. This is something for you to consider if you are energy sensitive or are a creature of habit.

Your Reiki Practice

A Space of Your Own

At about the year mark, as my practice grew, I yearned for a space of my own. This fit in well with my plan, as I was going to give myself a year and see how things went.

I took a shot at creating my own space. I was successful at it and was there for a little over a year, but I found it was not a good fit for me. It was more expensive, more work, and I found that I got lonely. I am very social, and like to interact with my co-workers. This was not an option when I had my own space. Often I would be at the center from morning to evening and while clients came and went I had a lot of down time, and got lonely.

I also was responsible for furnishing the entire space and paying all of the bills. My practice thrived during this time and I could afford it, so it wasn't that, rather I longed to be part of a group. I was grateful when I received the call from my old work group asking me to come back. I ran! I remember saying at the time "I just want to teach and practice Reiki!" All of that other responsibility and expense was just too much for me.

Independent Practitioner

After a few years of trial and error, I found what worked best for me. That was being an independent practitioner, as part of a larger group. In the acupuncture clinic where I subleased space I had my own room, my own business, and I was my own boss. Yet I was able to interact with other practitioners and we would trade services and clients. It was a win/win for all of us. It was social and fun, and I liked being part of a thriving clinic, with clients in the waiting room and a busy, upbeat air about the place.

Reiki Room in Your Home

I've always kept (and still do) a Reiki room in my home. It doubles as my office and I consider it a sacred space. This is where I see family and friends and a few clients.

It is a great arrangement, as you don't have to leave your home to go to work. On snow days, it is a blessing! I like it and I no longer worry about bringing clients into my home. If you have the space and are so inclined, I highly recommend it.

Working in a Medical Center

After I moved to Arizona, I began to practice Reiki at a medical center, working with cancer patients. Once again I found myself creating a position from scratch, this time a Reiki position. It was a wonderful opportunity and one of my favorite gigs to date. I was able to introduce Reiki to a population that really needed it.

Many of the patients there had never heard of Reiki and I loved sharing it with them. Watching them heal and thrive as a result of their sessions was both reassuring and fulfilling. At the two-year mark, after the program was up and running I left to work in my private practice and to write. Another Reiki Master has taken over and the program continues.

Initially it was offered as a volunteer position. I felt that would be a good way for me to keep up my Reiki, meet new people, and get my foot in the door. I consider every Reiki opportunity that comes my way, paid or not. You just never know. When I finally went for the interview I was delighted and surprised when they offered it as a paid position. Even better!

I was a contract employee and was paid through a foundation of the center, which I billed every two weeks. I saw patients that were going through chemo or radiation, 2-3 times per week. A secretary booked the appointments and the room was fully furnished. Much like the gym, all I had to do was show up and give Reiki.

There are so many different ways you can practice. Think about where you are in your career, how you see yourself working, your work style and your personality. Then go out and do it. I found that I was pretty much afraid in all of these scenarios, but did it anyway. It's great when we can get over ourselves.

Volunteer Opportunities

Maybe you want to do Reiki but for whatever reason you are not ready to practice professionally. If this is you I highly recommend that you volunteer to give Reiki. In Wisconsin, where I first began my Reiki career, there were many opportunities to do this. Most of them are not paid positions, but the work and the experience you receive will be priceless. Hospice centers, hospitals and community centers are a good place to begin. Check out your community and see what is available.

Naming Your Practice

How do you name your practice? Do you have a name in mind? Does it accurately describe what you do? Do you love it? Does it feel like you? What do you want the world to see or think when they see your business name? Ask yourself these questions when coming up with a name.

In this area, I trusted my guidance. I never took any business classes that taught this and wasn't sure how to go about it, so I asked for guidance, while meditating, and I got it. Do what works for you. If you have a name, great. If you don't do some research or ask *your* guidance. It will come to you in some way, shape of form.

It's important to listen. You might hear something you didn't expect.

When I first started and because I hadn't yet found a name that resonated with me I called my business Reiki Healing with Deb Karpek. This made sense to me. The name told people who'd be doing the work and that Reiki Healing was what I'd be doing. I thought it simple and straightforward, if lacking in creativity. I also liked having my name in it so old friends, classmates, and co-workers would recognize it and maybe come and see me if they were thinking about a Reiki session. It worked. Many people that were no longer in my life showed up in my practice when they discovered I was now doing Reiki. It was a great advertising tool.

After a while a name began appearing to me. It would drop in, unannounced, out of the blue and repeat itself like a mantra: Peaceful World, Peaceful World, Peaceful World. I realized this was what I was supposed to name my business, yet I resisted. And it persisted. And I resisted.

I resisted because I worried. I worried because Peaceful World was the name of a bar I used to sneak into when I was 17. The drinking age was 18 at that time. It was the summer after I graduated high school, and my boyfriend had just gone into the Navy. I was sad and lonely and wasn't looking forward to summer, as I normally did.

I began hanging out with my girlfriends and when we heard about this groovy new hippie bar that had opened up down the street, we decided to give it a whirl. We got in without being carded and it became our home away from home. In this place we were able to fly our freak flags for real! Peaceful World was the place to be in the summer of '72!

I loved the name and the energy of the place and I said at the time that if I ever owned a business it would be called Peaceful

World. I couldn't think of a better name! Yet when I began my business it didn't come to me, not for at least 5 or so years. Why not?

Because I don't believe that I was comfortable enough telling people who I really was. I think I was still trying to be my teacher, or anyone other than me. I wanted to be thought of as serious and I worried about the hippie connotations this name would conjure up. I no longer felt the freedom that my seventeen-year-old self felt that summer of '72. Instead, my ego was actively engaged and I worried.

When that mantra began popping into my head I realized I was ready to personalize the name of my business. Still I worried. Not so much about what people would say. Over the years Reiki had led me back to myself and I was quite comfortable flying my freak flag. Instead I worried that people wouldn't know what my business was. What if they thought it was a bar? In a moment of divine guidance I heard Peaceful World Reiki. I changed the name and I never looked back! It felt right and I'm very happy with it.

What will your business name be? Don't be afraid to share your light with the world. Let them know who you are!

Why Would Anyone Come to See You?

Why not? When we ask ourselves that question, it's a red flag that we are operating out of ego and fear. I've had so many of my students tell me that they cannot imagine doing healing work. I had a woman say to me the other day "Why would anyone come to see me?"

I had to laugh because I have felt the same way, many, many times. And not only when I was just starting out. Every once in a while that thought floats into my mind. Now I know that it's just ego and fear and not real at all but I really believed it in the beginning. As do so many of those who ask me.

Why would anyone come to see us, and what do we do with them when they do? I think this might be what scared me the most in the beginning. The reality of doing the work I trained to do. The reality of doing the work I'd longed to do. It was time to face the music.

It's one thing to go through the training and to think of yourself doing healing work. It's quite another thing to make the transition to actually doing it. Like any job you will go through a type of training, but here you will be training yourself. You will take what you learned in class and apply it to your practice, both in the Reiki room and in your classes. Making this transition was probably the hardest thing for me to do.

You just have to show up and do it. Find your way. Practice, practice, practice. Fake it until you make it. Keep putting one foot in front of the other and keep moving forward. Yes, these are all clichés but really this is the way you will learn. It's the only way to learn Reiki—by doing it. It will guide you and teach you, so listen.

I believe the people that find us are meant to work with us. They are attracted to our vibration. There could be two of us working side by side and we would attract those clients that desire our vibe. There is no competition in Reiki. I believe this with all my heart and when I share this with my students some do and many do not. I frequently get calls from new practitioners wanting to know why someone else got a client they thought they should get. I don't know.

I just trust that it's the way it's supposed to be. If you can do this it will save you a lot of heartache, jealousy and fear. I'm not a terribly competitive person and I was taught that we can't get people to come to us-that it's up to them-so this took a whole lot of pressure off. I just needed to get myself out there and trust that people would come. They have. It's as simple as that. Get out of your own way. Stop thinking about it and stop trying to control it. It just is. Know that you will help the people that are drawn to you.

It's the same thing when you've been working with someone for a while and they decide to stop and/or go to someone else. It's time. They are being guided on a higher level. Again, there's not much you can do about it, so learn to roll with it. Don't take it personally. I admit when this happened in the early years it would scare me (what didn't?) but I had to learn to heal that. I had a sincere desire to get over this and Reiki helped me to do that, sometimes using other practitioners to help me!

Ask Reiki to help you to get over your fears and to get out of your own way. If you have a sincere desire to do Reiki allow your clients to find you. They will. I promise.

Who Do You Wish to Work With?

Quite the opposite of *Why would anyone come to see me?* is *Who do you wish to work with?* Have you thought about this? What demographic you are most comfortable with? Think about whom you've worked with in your professional life or if there is a particular group that you'd like to work with in your Reiki practice. Do you have an idea of what that demographic looks like?

I didn't. I hadn't a clue. I just jumped right in and allowed it to flow, without too much thought. As I've repeated throughout this book if I had given that much attention to my business I would not have gone through with it. It was such a big thought and it scared me too much to go there. Instead I listened to my guidance as it appeared and then took action.

Still many of you *do* know whom you want to practice with. I have many students that practice Reiki only on animals. They work in Vets offices and their business is all about animals. This is who they are and they know it. I love that they have been able to achieve their dreams.

I know other students who prefer to work with children and teenagers. This is a demographic they work with in their professional lives and it has flowed into their Reiki practice. While they may have some adult clients they are most comfortable practicing and teaching a younger clientele.

Still others enjoy working with elderly adults, cancer and end of life or hospice patients. This is their calling and they are most comfortable with these groups.

While I've worked with all of the above, I am most comfortable with women around my own age, women in transition. This is whom I seem to attract to my practice. I can relate to them, understand them and delight in working with them. I don't think it is a coincidence that 90 percent of my clients fit that description.

If you are still not sure or don't really have any idea of who you'd like to work with, just ask Reiki. You'll find out soon enough.

How Many People Should You See in a Day/Week?

This is different for everyone. When I started, my magic number was 11 clients per week. The most Reiki treatments I do in a day is four, but I prefer to do only three.

I've had others tell me that they do more, like five or six in a day. I've never really been able to do that. At times I wished I could, for financial and scheduling reasons, but I always seem to come back to three.

In the client section that follows this, I talk about how I set my schedule and pace my day. Think about how and when you like to work, your energy level and what you are comfortable with. Start slow and build your way up. Don't get in over your head and don't be fixated on the financials. While we do have a to make a living, don't schedule more than you can handle just to make a certain amount of money. It won't be worth it.

Respect Reiki, your time and your client's session.

What Do You Do During a Session?

OK, you have your space, your business name, you've got a few clients and now it's time to practice. What do you do with yourself during that hour you are giving Reiki?

I've had so many people say to me "what do you do during a session?" or "how do you stay so still?" They think they won't be able to focus on Reiki for an hour or not be able to hold the hand positions and be still enough.

I'll be honest, when I first started practicing, I didn't focus much on the Reiki. I wasn't able to. It was all I could do to show up! I couldn't believe I was doing this. It seemed unreal that someone would pay me, that people would sign up for appointments, that I was doing healing work. Do all new practitioners feel this way or was I just super insecure and afraid?

So what do I do while working on a client? At the very beginning I was still working part-time as a conference planner so I planned my conferences in my head. It was hard for me, both physically and mentally to stand still for an hour and do Reiki, with two or three clients in a row. So my mind would wander and I would think of my other job. I never worried that the client would pick up on this, as I knew that Reiki flowed through me, and not from me. I was channeling Reiki, not my energy.

After a while, I learned how to listen to their bodies and get into a more meditative state. It took some time and practice, but now I am able to plug into them, go to that place of no thought, and be in the flow. But don't worry about any of this. Just put your hands on the person and get out of the way. Everything else will fall into place. Give it time and practice. Practice, practice, practice! Have I mentioned how important it is to practice?

Ergonomics

While you are giving a session, pay attention to your body and how you are using it. Probably the most difficult thing for me in the early sessions was the ergonomics of doing Reiki. I never thought about this when I started, and my body paid for it. Because I had so much going on in my head in the beginning, I didn't pay attention to my body. For starters, I never wore shoes when I first started practicing. I was so excited to be able to work barefoot! After about a year I developed some foot issues and the shoes went back on. Sensible shoes. That helped.

I also used to lean over the body and sort of tense my muscles as I held each hand position. I don't think I was even aware that I was doing this. I developed neck, shoulder and back pain as a result. This was an opportunity for me to begin paying attention to my body. Prior to this I don't think I ever did that while I worked.

I'm wound pretty tight and have always had terrible posture. Having sat hunched over a desk for most of my career I wasn't used to being on my feet all day and using my body in this new way. Reiki drew my attention to this and I began getting regular chiropractic care and massages. This has helped tremendously.

I brought a stool and an ergonomic chair into the Reiki room and used both. I am able to sit for most of the session and to use the table to brace my arms and legs (while standing). This new way of working at the table is much more gentle on my body.

Save your body the wear and tear and pay attention to how you use your body when working. I end each day with an Epsom salt soak in a hot bath. It helps draw out any toxins, is good for your muscles and skin and a great prelude to sleep. Love your body!

Reiki Shares

Reiki Shares are a great educational tool for yourself and your students. For a few years, I hosted Reiki Shares for my students. Once a month on a Sunday afternoon, I opened up the clinic to my students. I would have three to four tables to work with and 12 to 15 students would show up. We'd start the Share with introductions and a brief meditation, led by myself or one of the students. We'd then split up into groups of three or four and begin the Share.

I never participated. I preferred to be the organizer and timekeeper. Each person got about half an hour on the table and everyone got the chance to give and get Reiki. At the end of the practice part, we'd get back together and share our experiences. We'd end with another short meditation.

This was such a great learning experience. Even though I had trained all of these students, it was interesting to see the differences in how they approached Reiki. I'm fond of saying that when I teach, I lay the foundation for Reiki and each student builds his or her own house. This was very apparent at the Shares. All the students had their own unique ways of practicing and I loved how we all learned from one another.

Many of the students made connections in this group and got together to have smaller Shares of their own. This is not only a good opportunity to share Reiki, but a valuable networking opportunity as well. We met as a group for a few years, until the space was no longer available to us.

There are other types of Reiki Shares to which you can invite the public, but I have never participated in or hosted those. My intent was to use the Share as a continuing education tool for the students. If you are interested in the other type of Share, check out what your community has to offer.

Going to a community Share is also an excellent opportunity to meet other Reiki people and get into the flow. You never know whom you will meet and how they may be able to help you get started. And you get Reiki! Win/win!

QUESTIONS TO PONDER
CHECKLIST

☐ Are you overwhelmed by the thought of starting a Reiki practice? Think of it as "just another job." What skill sets do you have that you can use in this new job? What do you bring to the table?

☐ Naysayers! Are you troubled by them? Do you listen to them? Do you believe them and allow them to hold you back? Make a list of the naysayers in your life, along with your other triggers in this area.

☐ Can you recognize your fear of starting your practice? In what ways does it show up? Draw up a list of your fears and let them motivate you. Use them to your advantage.

☐ Where should you practice? What is your work style? Personality? Financial situation? Think about what type of workplace you are best suited for.

☐ Do you have a name in mind for your practice? Does it accurately describe what you do? Do you love it? Does it feel like you? Noodle around with some names until one feels right. Trust your gut.

☐ Who do you wish to work with? Think about what demographic you are most comfortable with. What experience do you have with a particular group you'd like to continue on with in your Reiki practice?

☐ How many clients would you like to work with in a day/week? Think about your energy level and when you like to work.

☐ Be mindful of your body while practicing Reiki. How can you make your practice more body-friendly?

☐ Start attending Reiki Shares in your community and consider creating one of your own.

The Business Side

I want to preface this section and say that these are my experiences, my stories, and what has worked for me. If any of this resonates with you, great. Use it as a starting point for your practice. I feel that most of this information is common sense, but I have been asked these questions so many times by my clients and students that I felt it was important to include them in the book.

Again, I ask you to think about what *you* bring to your business. What experience do you have, from past jobs and other things you've done in your life? Remember, this is really just one more job; treat it that way. Use all of your skill sets, creativity and smarts to grow your Reiki practice. And use your Reiki!

As I've mentioned, prior to coming to Reiki, I worked in corporate America. I started as a secretary, worked my way up to administrative assistant/office manager and ended my career as a conference planner. I was good at organizing and multi-tasking and I enjoyed my work.

For many years I sat in meetings, taking minutes. I was exposed to a lot of business practices among high-level professionals. I am forever grateful for this as it gave me a solid foundation when I began my business.

I was a nine-to-five, Monday-to-Friday type of worker. For the most part, I liked what I did and was good at it. Yet as I got older I had the sense that something was missing. I remember driving to work and wondering if this was all there was? I had a yearning to do something more, yet I wasn't sure what that "more" was.

That "more" came in the form of Reiki. I wasn't really sure I wanted to have a business but I knew I wanted to do Reiki. I will now share the things I did to develop my Reiki practice.

Reiki Samplers and Talks

I began my Reiki career as part of a spa in a health club. I'm very grateful I was guided to this as it made a lot of sense. I could keep my part-time job, work a few four-hour blocks a week at the gym, and, I had a built-in audience. I learned how to give talks to this community, as well as monthly "Reiki Samplers," which introduced Reiki to a population that may not have normally found it. I seem to attract a lot of Reiki newbies. The samplers and the talks were not my idea—rather they were a condition of my employment.

Once a month I set up a table outside of the Reiki room, with information about Reiki. I had brochures, cards and flyers. I also had a sign up sheet, with appointments every twenty minutes over a two-hour period. I was fortunate that the marketing department would post announcements prior to the event, so I usually had people waiting to sign up. If it got slow I'd go out into the gym and introduce myself. This was hard to do, as I was shy talking about Reiki, so it was a good learning/healing experience. Again, Reiki was helping me to get over myself.

Sometimes I would do the sampler with the client in a chair, and other times, the client would be on the table. I discovered that most folks preferred the chair as the table seemed too intimate for a sampler.

Once seated in the chair, I'd lower the lights, play soothing music and get to work. Folks relaxed immediately and gave themselves over to the Reiki. From that first Reiki sampler I got many new clients, some that stayed with me for years and some that are still with me.

Think of places in your community where you can give talks on Reiki or Reiki samplers. How can you get yourself and Reiki out there?

For the first three months, I gave a monthly Reiki talk. I kept the talk to an hour and focused on the basics. Because I came from a meeting planner background and I'm a Virgo, I generally over-prepare for things. In this case I typed up my speech and put it in a binder. I used the binder as a sort of safety net. I pretty much knew my material but in case I got nervous and forgot all I had to do was look down. It gave me something to hold on to, which made me feel safe.

While I was setting up, both for the samplers and the talk, I placed the Reiki symbols in the room, to clear and set sacred space. I played Reiki Chants by Jonathan Goldman softly in the background. This is such a great CD for raising the vibration of a space. I find people respond to it without conscious awareness. It can be very relaxing and healing.

Community Talk Template

Below is a basic outline you can use as a template when giving talks in the community. I encourage you to develop your own, but this may help get you started.

What is Reiki? A Brief Overview

- ❐ Introduce yourself, provide a brief bio
- ❐ Definition of Reiki
- ❐ What Reiki Is and Isn't
- ❐ What a Reiki session can do for you
- ❐ What to expect from a Reiki session
- ❐ The Reiki Principles

- ❏ Brief Chakra Overview
- ❏ History of Reiki
- ❏ Demonstration (Use someone from the audience. Put in a chair at front of room.)
- ❏ Q&A

Offer samplers after the talk or at another pre-arranged time. I had a sign-up sheet in the room, as there wasn't time after the talk. While the above agenda looks ambitious, there is no need to go into great detail - just skim the surface and give them the basic facts. If you can talk and do head samplers at the same time do it, as people better understand Reiki if they can feel it. And it's okay to be nervous—ask Reiki to help you with your fear and just Do It Afraid!

Business Plan
(Having a Plan vs. Having a Clue)

About a year into my business a colleague asked me if I had a solid business plan. She said I could not start a business without one. Since I had already been working for about a year, I wondered how that could be. I stated that I did not have one, but I did have a sort of plan.

Instincts and intuition were my plan. I told her that and she laughed at me! She told me I would fail quickly if I didn't have a solid business plan. She said I was flying by the seat of my pants and it wouldn't go well. She made some negative comments about my being "woo-woo" and again told me I was setting myself up for failure.

I understood her concern, even if I was turned off by her insistence of my future failure. I also agree that most businesses do need a plan. Yet, I never felt the need to do this. Did I read books on how to start a business? Yes. Did I write up a sort of plan? Yes. Did I attend seminars on how to run a business? Yes. I knew what I wanted and I had a vague idea about how to go about it.

Use Your Guidance

I don't mean that you shouldn't take your business seriously. I did. I just did it differently. I have very strong guidance. And even though I came from a planning type of background and am a planner at heart I didn't plan a lot when it came to my business.

Instead I waited for and listened to the guidance when it came. And it always came, as evidenced in some of the other stories in this book. And it has paid off.

I'm a big fan of creative visualization. I made a vision board when I first began my business. I "saw" what I wanted for my practice and I cut out pictures to represent that vision on my board. I then sat with my board daily, giving it Reiki, meditating. I "felt" what it would be like to have a thriving Reiki practice. And eventually it came to fruition.

I made one giant vision board to include not only my Reiki practice, but also all of my life goals. At the time of making the board, I wasn't sure it was possible to have all of this but I surely wanted it and believed in the power of positive visualization, combined with Reiki. Now, all these years later, I have everything on that board, with the exception of the million-dollar bill. However, my relationship with money has evolved into a healthy one. Try it, it works!

Affirmations

I also used affirmations. Every day on my commute to work, I employed the Reiki distance symbol (HSZSN) and asked for what I wanted in a practice. One of my very first affirmations went something like this:

"I have a thriving Reiki practice. I see 11 clients per week. I work in a safe, clean, and affordable environment with co-workers that are loving and respectful. I make an abundant living doing what I love."

I did this for about six months and within a year, I had my 11 clients per week and kept that going until I moved to Arizona seven years later. Eleven was the perfect number for me at the time. I found a safe, clean, affordable environment with wonderful co-workers.

Do What Works for you, But Do It

In retrospect, I see that a big reason I didn't plan too much is that I also had a large amount of fear about doing this. I felt if I thought about it too much I would get scared and not do it. So I didn't. Instead I trusted my intuition and tried to be in the flow as much as I was able to be at that time. This is what worked for me. You know what you need, so give yourself that.

Trust your instincts and guidance. Others mean well, and do listen to their advice, but if it does not resonate with you, you don't need to take it. You will know what to do. Don't let others' expectations and values determine yours.

Listen To That Voice in Your Head

I can't stress enough how important it is to follow your guidance and trust your gut. This is how I was led to begin my business. From first finding Reiki at that Women's Wellness Conference to starting my gig at the gym, to getting my first space, to going out on my own and back to that original space-all of this came from my guidance.

I tell my students to listen to that voice, especially if it does not sound like your mind. That voice is your guidance. For so many years I heard that voice and thought it was my anxiety, that mindless chatter in my head. Because it was so different from how I thought, I did not take it seriously. I wish I had.

I remember times it had told me to leave a relationship, to end a friendship, to go to a conference, to not go on a trip, and I never listened. I wonder how different things would be had I listened those times.

But many times I did listen and it's proven to be just what I needed when I needed it. There is a saying about Reiki; *Reiki finds you when you need it and it gives you what you need.* Guidance is like that as well. I guess it might be safe to say that Reiki gave me back my guidance. It allowed me to plug in and trust.

So do what works for you, just be sure to educate yourself, do your homework, listen to your guidance, and don't forget to ask Reiki!

Insurance
Once you start practicing Reiki on others, even if it is only in your home, be sure to get insurance. I've used both IARP.com and Reikimembership.com. as places to get my insurance. Both are inexpensive with the needed coverage. Don't scrimp here—it will protect you. If you are practicing outside of the home, your landlord will require it. The type of insurance I have (through the above venues) covers wherever you practice.

Limited Liability Company (LLC)
Should you form an LLC for your business? I believe this is a personal decision. When I first started my business, I looked into it

but decided to wait a bit. I wasn't sure where I was going with it and didn't want to spend the money, as I didn't know if I was going to continue. I know a few colleagues that did this and then abandoned their dream/business. I didn't want to do that.

About a year after I left the spa and went out on my own, I thought it might be time to form an LLC. I looked into it again and I just didn't feel the need. I know that practitioners are better protected when they have an LLC. If anything happens, your personal worth is not affected. Still, knowing this I wasn't guided to do it. After a while, I just forgot about it and at this point, I don't feel it is necessary for me.

Sole Proprietor

I file my taxes jointly with my husband as a sole proprietor. I use my Social Security Number (SSN) as my tax ID number and I report my earnings. So far this has served me well. Do your homework, check out the opportunities available, and see what speaks to you and your needs. Trust your gut.

Accounting

While I am a Virgo and quite organized, I also believe in keeping things simple, especially in matters of tracking my expenses. Again, I am sharing what I've done and what works for me. I'm sure there are more efficient ways of doing this, but I find my method simple and effective. There are many good software packages you can purchase or you may want to consider hiring someone to do your books if you are not comfortable doing them yourself. Do what works for you, but do something.

I keep all of my appointments on a hand-written calendar. (Yes, I am "old school.") I also have a back-up calendar at home. On this back-up calendar, I record my income. At the end of the month, I tally up my income, the number of clients I saw, and how many classes I taught. I put this information into an Excel spreadsheet.

I keep a monthly file for all of my expenses. I put all receipts into the file of the month I purchased it. At the end of the month, I tally up my expenses, separating into categories—rent, supplies, furniture, printing, marketing, insurance, professional organizations, etc.

Create your own list of what you spend your money on to keep your business running. I put this information into the same Excel spreadsheet as my income.

At the end of the year, the spreadsheet tallies everything. I give my tax person (my husband) a list of the income, expenses, and net income. It really is as simple as that.

To keep it as simple as this, be sure to enter your information into the spreadsheet on a monthly basis. Waiting until the end of the year is time-consuming and one big hassle. Trust me, I've done it.

Marketing

Early in my Reiki career, I was interviewed for an article about Reiki for a local magazine. When the writer called to ask me if she could set up a time, I asked her "why me?" There were plenty of Reiki folks in our community with lots more experience than I had. She said it was because everywhere she went she saw my name. She figured it *had* to be me! That made me smile, as it seemed my marketing efforts were paying off.

I use traditional methods, as most of the practices below attest to. When I first began my Reiki practice in 2005, Facebook didn't exist and I wasn't aware of any social media, so I relied on these conventional ways. It's only been recently that I've begun to dip my toe in the social media pond and am considering creating more of an online presence. Still, these methods seem to have worked well for me—and my clients like them. It is my intention to create a hybrid of the old and the new to stay relevant and in the flow. Bottom line—do what works for you.

Below are some examples of how I got my name and business out there.

Business Cards

In the beginning, I made my own business cards with card stock. Unless you are really creative and have the experience, I wouldn't recommend this. I didn't want to put out the money, and so I did my own. In retrospect, I see that they looked cheap and unprofessional. The good thing about this is I had cards right away and I could change them as I saw fit. If you are good at design, you might try this to start out. This was not my strong suit.

After about a year, I discovered Vistaprint.com. All these years later I still use them. I like their templates and the price is right: almost free! You pay for shipping and you can upgrade them for a small cost. There are many templates and they are made with decent card stock.

Don't spend a lot of money on cards. They are throwaway items; I don't care what anyone says. (And there are many opinions about this.) How many cards do you save when you get them? I've got a desk drawer full of them and I don't remember who half of the people are. Maybe it's just me but I never really pay attention to things like design, font and layout. I look for the name, email, phone and website. Make those easy to read and you'll be fine.

Promotional Items

Over the years I've used many promotional items but my personal favorites are the pens. I purchase pens in bulk and give them away at every opportunity. I like the basic stick pen, in tie dyed colors. There are bright and fun and fit well with my personality! I hand them out in class, the first time I meet a client for a session (along with a brochure and card), at fairs, and to potential clients, as it has my contact info on them. Who doesn't need and want a pen?

Another item I used early on was a magnetic card or calendar with my contact info. Clients love getting these and they are fun to give away. In the end, however, the pens won out. I order the pens from Pens.com and the magnetic cards and calendar are from Vistaprint.com.

Brochures

I am proficient in Word, so I created my own brochures. I went around town and collected the brochures of other Reiki Masters and massage therapists. I used them to get an idea of what I wanted to say and how to lay it out. I'd never done anything like this and wasn't sure what to do so this really helped. I discovered things on others' brochures that I would not have thought of.

I liked the idea of having a feedback section and I felt it was important to have my picture. I like it when other's put their photo on their brochures. I can get a feel for someone's energy from his or her photo. I also wrote a short bio, and included information about classes and rates, and of course, a brief description of Reiki. I wanted it to look well balanced and not busy. I don't think it's super-professional, but I actually liked that, because I wanted a down-to-earth look.

Nor did I want to spend a lot of money on the brochure. I found a local neighborhood printer with good rates and would get copies printed up every so often for a very good price. When I had to use the bigger box printing places, it could get quite expensive. Once in a while I would print a few from my printer at home, but that is not very cost effective.

If you are a member of the Reiki Membership Association (www.reikimembership.com), one of the perks is a brochure that you can use and personalize.

Rack Cards

After moving to Arizona I noticed that rack cards seem to have replaced brochures as a mode of advertising one's business. I'm not sure if this is geographic or a sign of the times or both. I recently decided to retire my brochures and have created my first rack card using a template on Vistaprint. I love it! It captures all of the basics of the brochure, but is less cumbersome. I am thinking that it's a much more effective marketing tool, as there isn't so much copy to read. If someone is interested they can call, email or check out my website. Evolution!

Postcards

Postcards are a great marketing tool. I have used them to advertise pricing specials, to remind clients to come get some Reiki, for the holidays and just because. You can make your own with the many programs out there or again use Vistaprint.com. This is the route I've always taken, as it is fast, easy and inexpensive. Feedback from clients has been very positive. My clients love getting fun snail mail! I've also used them to advertise on bulletin boards in the community. They are bigger than business cards but smaller than rack cards. They really stand out. This is probably my most favorite marketing tool. Try it!

Flyers & Newsletters

I like to write and I like to stay connected to my clients so early in my career I started a quarterly newsletter. I used it to list upcoming classes and also added some personal information about what I'd been up to. My clients responded well to the newsletter, even looked forward to it.

There was usually a theme, tied to a holiday. I added coupons to be cut out and brought in for a session. This worked out very well. People in the Midwest love coupons! I thought about putting my newsletter online but I received such positive feedback that I continue to send it via snail mail. I love getting snail mail that is fun, as do many of my clients. These flyers were also distributed throughout the community, and I kept a stack of them in my office.

Marketing

When I moved to Arizona, I was asked to continue these newsletters, so I did. Every eight weeks or so, I send one out. Because of this, I've been able to keep a large portion of my Wisconsin practice. I teach there a few times a year and practice when I go back in the summer. The classes and practice times are always listed in my newsletter. I've gotten such positive feedback so I've kept it going. I always feel shy, like "*why would anyone care about what I'm doing*" and I worry that it sounds braggy, but my clients say that they love it. And I love that it keeps me connected to then. Win/win.

Email List
Keep an email list of all of your clients. Not only do I send out the snail mail newsletters (my clients enjoy this), I also stay in touch with them via email. I send out articles, updates, upcoming class information, holiday wishes, anything I can think of to stay in touch. I get email addresses from class lists or the Client Information Form they fill out on their first visit. However you do it, it's important to stay in touch with your clients.

Website
When I first stated my practice it didn't even occur to me to have a website. Most of my business came from word of mouth. I did place a few ads in local magazines and had my flyers and cards all over the area and I thought this was enough.

In the second year of my practice I met a young man who developed websites. He suggested I needed one and I just shrugged it off; I didn't take his suggestion seriously. It wasn't for my demographic I thought. How would a website serve me? He became a regular Reiki client and every so often he would remind me about the website. After a while I began to take him seriously and realized he was right. He offered me a deal I could not refuse and I began to think about what I wanted.

I wrote the copy for the website. I had a lot of it written already from articles I planned on sending to *Reiki News Magazine* and I also took some info from my brochures and other marketing material I had. As far as the design, I told him what I would like it to look like but pretty much gave him free rein to design it based on what I wanted. I wanted it to be clean, classy and easy to navigate. He did an amazing job.

Speaking of amazing, I cannot believe how lucrative the site has been! Almost immediately people began contacting me about Reiki. It didn't occur to me that people would google "Reiki in Franklin" and my name would come up. It did! A lot! I am so grateful to that young man for suggesting it, for being persistent and then coming up with an amazing site. I am now living in Arizona and I have clients that drive up north from Phoenix to see me for sessions and classes because they found me from my website. So get a website. Do it yourself, or pay someone to do it, just do it. You won't regret it. In this day and age, your website is your storefront. Make it easy to navigate, informative and accessible. This is your snapshot of *you*, so be sure it reflects who you are and what you do.

Social Media

I have to admit I was slow to board this train. When I began my business in 2005, I don't think there was much in the way of social media, at least not that I was aware of.

Facebook

When I did finally get on Facebook it was because of my Reiki practice. I had no real desire to be on this site but I thought (and I was right) it would be an excellent marketing opportunity.

In the beginning I did not set up a page for my practice. Instead I did a personal page and talked a lot about getting Reiki and taking classes. I connected with many co-workers of years past and even some high school friends who have ended up being long-term clients. After a few years I created a business page and now I use both to advertise my practice. Facebook is free and far-reaching, but I'm sure you already know about that.

LinkedIn

I have used LinkedIn much the same way I use Facebook to advertise my practice. The bonus for me is that many of my LinkedIn friends are not on Facebook, so I am reaching a larger audience. Again, it is free and far-reaching, so if you don't have an account, get one.

Twitter, Instagram, YouTube, etc.

I've yet to use any of these and at this point, am just considering it. I'm in a different place with my practice than when I first began my business. I now consider myself semi-retired and work about half as much as I used to. Because of this, I advertise about half as much. However, if I were just starting out I would use every avenue of social media available. You should, too. It's there and it's free, and once again, it's far reaching. Get your business out there!

Print Ads in Magazines and Newsletters

Early on in my career I used print ads in magazines and newsletters from other organizations. It took a while for them to pay for themselves but eventually they did in spades. A local health food co-op had a monthly magazine and I bought a small ad for years. It took a while for people to begin calling but once they did they never stopped. I read somewhere that people need to see your name a number of times before they respond to it.

It's my belief that when you advertise for any length of time, it comforts people, helps them to believe you are serious and steady. I am and I was. I got so many of my clients from this publication. It was a good demographic fit for me as well.

I also paid for a small ad in a regional women's magazine and twice a year purchased a profile in the same magazine. Again, the magazine was a good demographic fit. As I said it took a while for these ads to generate income but once they did it never stopped. I also felt it helped to have my name in more than one (but similar) magazine, as it got multiple looks.

Word of Mouth

The very best advertising is word of mouth. I can trace back more than half of my practice from one or two of my original clients. Think about it-when you get good service you tell your friends and family. Reiki is no different. You get back what you give out so give good service and you will be rewarded with a thriving Reiki practice.

Remember this goes both ways-if you don't provide your client with the best you can give, not only will they not come back to you but they may share their experience with others. With social media you really don't want this happening. If something less than positive occurs in a session or a class please address it immediately. Take responsibility for your behavior and resolve the situation to the best of your ability.

Now here's what to do with these marketing items.

Marketing

Be Prepared

I keep a box in the back seat of my car and it is always filled with flyers, brochures, rack cards, postcards, business cards and thumbtacks. If I go to the health food store I check the bulletin board and if needed I add a brochure and some cards. If I go to the gym and someone asks me what I do for a living I can tell them and then run out to my car and get a brochure and card. If I am in a writing class, or any type of community gathering I always bring a few cards and brochures inside. I've gotten many clients this way.

Once I took a water aerobics class at my gym. I went into the hot tub after the class to relax and so did the class instructor. We started talking and I told her I did Reiki. She told me she was a massage therapist and our offices were not far from each other. Within a month, we were doing trades and this continued until I moved away. She also became a student, taking classes all the way through Karuna. You never know where there is a potential client. Talk about your business everywhere to everyone.

Stores

Our local grocery store (a big chain with lots of shoppers) has a huge bulletin board with local advertising. It is in a locked glass cabinet located at the front of the store. Everyone has to walk by it as they enter and exit. Flyers are displayed on a week-to-week basis and they were really good about letting me put a new flyer in every week. Again, this generated a few new customers.

I also went to the strip malls in my neighborhood, parked my car and walked in and out of the stores, meeting new people, asking for my flyers to be put up, and handing out my cards and brochures. It was a great way to educate people about Reiki and for the most part people were interested. It was also another opportunity to get over myself and Do It Afraid.

And boy, was I afraid! I was terrified! I feared rejection, being laughed at, or not being taken seriously. I discovered that this was my fear and not a reality. There were some who were not interested, but they were kind about it.

Most people did want to know about Reiki, as they'd never heard of it. It was helpful for me to hone my "elevator speech"— *What is Reiki?*—to just a few minutes. This was preparing me for the networking meetings I would soon be speaking at. I highly recommend doing this. You'll get your name out there and learn how to talk about Reiki in short bursts, and get new clients.

Doctors' Offices

I visited local doctors' offices and asked them if they would display my brochure. Many of these offices had racks advertising other practitioners and modalities. Here is another opportunity to meet new people and educate them about Reiki. Even if they don't agree to put your brochure out (but most did) you may get a client from the receptionist or other office personnel. I found Chiropractor and Physical Therapy offices to be the most receptive. Sometimes I would reciprocate and put their brochures and cards in my office. I love building community!

Health Fairs

Check out the local health fairs in your community and sign up for a table. Some charge a small entrance fee, but many do not. I did many of these and I really enjoyed them. I had a table filled with my cards, brochures, and flyers, as well as copies of magazines and/or newspapers articles about the benefits of Reiki.

Here is another great opportunity to introduce and teach people about Reiki. Even if they do not come to see you consider that you are planting a seed for them. I have found that it takes people a while to think about it before calling. They may call you months later or someone else but at least you are exposing them to a new healing modality. It's another great way to get your business out there.

Sometimes I would have my Reiki colleagues or a student come with me and one of us would talk and the other would do some hands on ten-minute Reiki samplers. This was how I had my first Reiki session and it changed my life. I never charged for these but I've seen other practitioners charge $1 per minute, letting people decide how long they wanted to receive Reiki.

I became part of my community's yearly Senior Health Fair. My name and business would be listed in the monthly newsletter the county sent out. This was another great (free) advertising opportunity, as the folks in my town would see my name over and over again, associated with a stable organization (the Health Department).

On occasion, I would have people come up to my table and tease me, if it were in a mall or other type of public place. These were usually younger folks, making fun of the Reiki, accusing me of voodoo. At first this made me really uncomfortable until I turned it around and used it as another teaching opportunity. Sometimes it worked, other times not so much and then it became an opportunity for me to get over myself!

Community Bulletin Boards

Many coffee shops, restaurants, and community centers have bulletin boards or areas for locals to display their cards. Don't be shy about getting yours out there. This is how I met my first Reiki Master. Her card was on a bulletin board in the co-op I frequented. While waiting in line to use the bathroom one day I was looking at the board and found her card. I wonder how different my life would be if I hadn't had to go to the bathroom that day?

Laundromats

I put my flyers and a stack of cards on the bulletin boards of local laundry mats. You have a captive audience here! To be safe, I asked for and got permission to put them up. More free advertising. Here again I got a few new customers. Try it, it works!

Community Outreach

Another unanticipated but very successful way to get my name and my business out there was through the local Parks and Recreation Department. Each semester I was scheduled to teach either a Reiki, Writing, or Vision Board class. My business name and said classes were printed in their catalog that went out a few times a year. It went to most of the homes in my community.

Sometimes the classes did not fill but everyone receiving the flyers would see my name and the name of my business in my bio. I couldn't pay for that type of advertising. This is another area that increased my name recognition and brought in business.

Memberships and
Professional Affiliations

Think about joining professional organizations. There is a cost involved, but the rewards are worth it. If you want to present yourself as a professional it is important to align yourself with other like-minded individuals and use the resources they offer. It also shows your clients and potential clients that you are serious and committed. It looks good to have those credentials after your name.

People respond to that. I know that it shouldn't make a difference but It does. It is important to do whatever you can to set yourself apart from the others in your field. Not everyone is aware of Reiki and some may have incorrect, pre-conceived ideas about Reiki and Reiki practitioners. They may feel more comfortable if they see you are affiliated with professional organizations and it might not seem as scary to them. It gives you and your business more recognition and credibility. Below are organizations I belong to, or have belonged to.

The Better Business Bureau

You can put their logo on your website, cards, brochures and flyers. You can also affix their logo to the front door of your business and hang their certificate in your office. I do not regret my decision to belong to this organization. Again it shows you are serious and lends credibility to you and your business and instills confidence in your potential clients when they are researching other Reiki practitioners.

National Certification Board for Therapeutic Massage and Bodywork (NCBTMB)

If you are going to teach Reiki I recommend you apply to become an Approved Provider for the National Certification Board for Therapeutic Massage and Bodywork. The application process is quite hefty, time consuming and somewhat expensive but it is worth your consideration. I did this early in my teaching career and going through the application process allowed me to really think about what and how I was going to teach. It was an excellent education for me. Being an Approved Provider means you are able to grant Continuing Education Credits to massage therapists.

Massage therapists make excellent Reiki students and practitioners. They are already doing healing work and are comfortable touching people. They get to further their practice and you will open yourself up to a whole new demographic. Once you are approved you name goes on their website and many new clients will find you. It's been my experience that they refer their colleagues as well. Once approved you are good for three years and the recertification process is inexpensive and easy.

The International Association of Reiki Professionals (IARP)

The International Association of Reiki Professionals is the first professional organization I joined. It is an excellent resource for the Reiki practitioner and teacher. If you teach you can get your certificates here. You can also buy your insurance through them. After much research I found them the least expensive with the best coverage. On their website there is a magazine and a library of Reiki articles. When you join you will receive a membership card and certificate for your wall and you will be able to participate in the many resources they provide.

Reiki Membership Association (RMA)

The Reiki Membership Association is a part of The International Center for Reiki Training (ICRT). Insurance, brochures, social networking, a class database and certificates are offered here, as well as an extensive Reiki Library. You receive a certificate for your wall and are able to partake in the various services offered.

Networking

Networking is an excellent way to get you and your practice out into the community. It can be scary but it is an effective, fun and smart way to market yourself.

I liked participating in these groups and it was a great way to not only market myself but to educate folks about Reiki, especially those who may not have heard or known about it. It has been my experience that most of these people are very open to it and many have booked appointments after I spoke with them.

Starting Small

I joined many networking groups. The first group I joined was perfect for a novice like myself. It was a small group of local, small business folks. We met once a month at the library and at each meeting there would be a guest speaker; someone from the group talking about their product. I never got up the courage to be the guest speaker, but I attended the meetings faithfully every month.

I learned how to talk about Reiki to people who had never heard of it. I learned how to promote myself. I felt very shy about this in the beginning but soon learned from the other people in the meeting how it was done. I developed some slogans "Come get some Reiki" and "Reiki finds you when you need it and it gives you what you need." In time I became more at ease with the process. I also gained a few clients from this group who are still with me to this day.

Chamber of Commerce

Through this networking group I was encouraged to join the local Chamber of Commerce. Even though it was somewhat expensive I felt it was worth it. It was another way to get my name out there. My name and contact information were put into their advertising booklet. I also took out a monthly ad for $25 and it was printed in their newsletter. This reached many people and I received many inquiries and some clients.

I went to a few of the social events but I felt I made more of an impact with the ads.

From this Chamber group, a sub-group was formed that consisted of other area Chambers. They met once a month for a luncheon/mixer. Even though it really wasn't my type of event, one day I was guided to go. I'm glad I did.

For that first visit, I dressed up and went alone. The first half hour was socializing, followed by a big lunch. After lunch, each person in the room was asked to speak about his or her business for three minutes. If you went over the time limit, a bell would ding. *And* we had to speak into a microphone!

I almost bolted after walking in the door. It was a big group in an even bigger room, set for about 100 people. The largest networking group I'd been to before this was about 15 people. I noticed there were very few women and most of the men were older, wore suits, and looked to be in sales. I was very much out of my comfort zone.

I spotted a table full of women and I joined them. We made small talk and enjoyed a nice lunch. Then the microphone appeared! It began on the other side of the room, which gave me sufficient time to work myself up into quite a lather. By the time it was handed to me for my three minutes I was sweating and shaking. I don't even remember what I said, but I'm sure it came out in squeaks. Talk about Doing It Afraid! I was so nervous. I don't remember much after I sat down, until the end of the meeting. It felt like a blackout.

After the meeting everyone was encouraged to mingle. I was collecting my business cards and brochures, preparing to leave, when a young man approached me. He told me that he, too, was a Reiki Master. This surprised me and immediately put me at ease. I had an idea in my head that everyone in the room was secretly making fun of me, that they all thought I was this spacey, hippie–type gal talking woo-woo. Of course, that was not true; it was my fear speaking, but it's how I felt.

The young man asked me if I liked teaching Reiki. I told him I loved to teach. He then gave me a lead; a local college was looking for a Reiki teacher. I thanked him and on my way out realized that this must have been why I was guided to go. I followed up on that lead and the next semester, I was teaching Reiki at a college in the University of Wisconsin system. I kept that gig for two years. You just never know when an opportunity is going to appear. Follow your guidance.

A few years after that first Chamber luncheon, I attended one of their holiday luncheons. I'd been going every few months since that first scary meeting. I got braver as I got to know folks, and I also sometimes brought a guest. Eventually many of my other network-ing sisters joined, so it became another social event. At this very festive Christmas luncheon when it was my turn to speak, I twirled the microphone and sang the opening words to *Volare*! You might say I'd gotten over my fear.

Other Groups

I joined more networking groups. There are so many different kinds of groups. Find one that fits you and your energy and do it. My favorite one was another smaller, women's group. We'd meet for lunch, visit with each other, enjoy a healthy meal and share about our businesses. I met many clients this way and it was a great social outlet as well. In the days where I was working all the time, it was a welcome respite in my week.

I've used all of the above networking methods, and I'm sure there are many more. Do whatever it takes to get your name out there!

Money

D o you have money issues? If you do, Reiki can help you to overcome them. If you aren't sure or aware that you might, you will certainly find out when you have your own business. There will be many opportunities for learning and healing. Be open to this.

I've learned so many things around the issue of money. I learned how to use my creativity around pricing for Reiki sessions and classes, how to handle the matter of payments, and how to lose my fear around money, which I believe stems from an old belief that I did not deserve it. I think this was inherited from my parents. We rarely discussed money and when we did, it was the lack of it, how we never had enough and never would. I grew up poor and money was seen as something others had, but not us.

I carried this belief into my adult life.

Most of my work life was spent in the corporate world. I went to work, did my job, and my paycheck was direct-deposited. About the only time I thought about money was at my yearly review when I received a raise. There wasn't much of a need to think or talk about it. When I first started practicing Reiki, I didn't charge anyone. I felt the "exchange" was my friends giving me their time and bodies to practice on. It was exciting and fun, and I set aside a Saturday morning every week to practice.

Sometimes friends and family would bring me baked goods or small tokens of appreciation, which I gratefully accepted. It felt good. My first paid Reiki job was at a health club as part of the spa.

The payments were handled by the front desk prior to the session. Occasionally a client would tip me. That was so hard for me to accept, as I had never been in a job where I received tips. It embarrassed me and I could barely look the person in the eye. I felt so shy! I'd try to discourage them and eventually I'd shove the money in my pocket, unable to look at it.

Now, while I don't expect them, tips delight me! I welcome them. So if your clients want to tip you, take the tip. You've earned it. They are telling you they are happy with your service. You deserve it.

When I left the health club and began my own practice, I came face to face with the issue of money, starting out with what to charge. Do I charge my family? Do I have a special friend rate? I didn't know many people in the Reiki business, so I did my research online and came up with a rate that seemed fair.

I also decided to have a coupon for first-timers—charging half price for the first session. I was criticized by some of my colleagues for not charging enough, but I trusted my instincts. I'm glad I did because it has been quite successful. I believe that the special rate brings in those first-time Reiki clients who have been on the fence. I have discovered that about 75 percent of those first-time clients return and become regulars.

So, in theory, I was comfortable with the money aspect. Face to face, it was different story. In the beginning of my practice, I felt very shy and uncomfortable asking for payment. I would wait until clients brought it up. If they didn't, I'd be distracted and worried about it. Sometimes it never came up, and I'd be chasing them out into the parking lot after the session, telling them I "forgot." This went on for a while until I decided to just Do It Afraid and ask for payment before the session.

Just like the gym personnel's policy, *I'd* take care of business first—get it out of the way so I could focus on the client.

Now, all these years later, I am more comfortable with the issue of money. I've done a lot of work in this area and have learned how and when to recognize my money triggers. For a while, I spent too much time focusing on what others charged and compared myself to them. I'd get angry if a student of mine charged too much starting out. I was jealous, if I'm honest. Then I'd worry about me not charging enough or thinking I didn't deserve it.

After much meditation, I've decided to trust my guidance. I now have a more flexible attitude toward the cost of my classes and sessions. I have a set price, but will use a sliding scale if needed. I rarely turn anyone away and try to find a price that serves every-one. My guidance is usually right on and I've learned to trust it in these money matters. Be aware of your triggers, know where you stand in regard to money, and be open to the healing opportunities that will flow your way. And flow they will!

How Much Should You Charge for Sessions?

This is probably one of the questions I get asked the most when people are starting their practice. It's a good question and the answer is different for everyone.

Before I began my practice, I looked at what other Reiki practitioners and energy and body workers charged in my area. It ran the gamut from $45/session to $80/session. I settled into what I considered to be a mid-way point. That was in 2006. Now it's 2016 and I live near Sedona, Arizona, where I see prices ranging from $45/session to $120/session. Again, I settled for something near the middle, and use a sliding scale for seniors, students, and anyone who might need the flexibility.

Money

In my practice, a session consists of an hour on the table and some talk time before and after. That differs with each client, but I can plan on about an hour and a half for most clients.

If clients buy a three-pack of sessions and pay up front, I give them a deal, with $10 off per session, which is a nice savings for them. It also helps them to keep their commitment to monthly Reiki.

I feel it is important to keep Reiki affordable. Many of my clients are single women, single parents, retired, sick, or people who don't have a lot of money. I'm happy to say I have the most loyal clients in the world. They come month after month, and buy three-pack after three-pack of sessions. I want to keep it affordable and allow them to keep coming back.

And to those critics, sure, I could have raised my rates, but I don't believe I would have had the large and loyal base that I do if I had done that. Others have criticized me saying that I didn't value myself and my low rates were indicative of that.

To the contrary, I felt that I was paying homage to Reiki by not inflating my prices and keeping it available to the masses. And the masses came. I have had a thriving Reiki practice for many, many years. My clients trust me, they are happy to pay my prices, and I can make an honest living from it. I also feel that my charging less is a form of community service.

In the end, you need to do what feels right to you. Be careful that you don't let your money issues get in the way of your pricing. I've seen people charge too much because they need the money, and not charge enough because they are afraid to. Ask Reiki to help you set your prices. Be aware of how it feels. Set your price and off you go!

How Much Should You Charge for Classes?

Good question. Again, the answer is different for everyone. It's another one of those questions that can bring up our stuff. For those of us with money issues, it can be a sticky one. The pricing for classes was harder for me than pricing for a session, because initially I had insecurity about my teaching abilities.

When I first started out, I had a tendency to charge less for classes because I was inexperienced. I researched what the going rate was for the levels of Reiki in my area and subtracted $25. At about the year mark, I raised my rate to match many of the rates in the area.

Recently a new teacher asked me this question and I told her not to undervalue herself and charge less because she has never taught Reiki. She teaches school for a living and has a lot of Reiki experience. I believe she is worth the full price. I believe we all are. The rate reduction I did in the beginning spoke more to my insecurities than about me being an inexperienced teacher. And while I had never taught before, I do believe I came to my classes prepared and in knowledge of the material.

Unless you are really guided to charge less, don't. Research other teachers in your area and price yourself accordingly. You'll know by how it feels if you have the right price. Meditate and ask Reiki. (Do you see a pattern here? Always ask Reiki.)

Coupons

A few times a year (quarterly), I mailed out coupons and specials to my clients. Some were focused around the holidays, others as a gift of gratitude. For the folks who had been with me a year or more, I'd send them a $25/off a three-pack. They loved getting snail mail (it's so old fashioned!) and most of them used the coupons. It not only kept them coming back, but it also showed them I appreciated their loyalty and continued presence. Gratitude is so important.

Bartering

Bartering can also be an option if the client has something you want to trade with. For years, I never paid for a massage or a haircut, as I bartered Reiki for those things. Everyone wins! However, be careful not to barter for something you do not want or otherwise would not do. Make sure it's something that is right for you. I rarely bartered for classes, but once in a while I made an exception if it was something I could really use. Trust your instincts. You'll know.

Scholarships

A few times a year, I offer scholarships for my students. Again, I am guided as to who will receive one. It's usually someone who has a desire to take a class and is walking the path, but is not able to afford the class. I believe it's a goodwill gesture and firmly believe in giving back. This is my way to do it. I do the same with sessions if I am so guided

I've taught classes to the patients at the cancer center where I worked. A few times a year, I offered Reiki Level One and Two to the patients, their caregivers and staff of the center. I lowered the prices considerably for this population and also offered scholarships, as these folks can really use Reiki. It has been a success and I am grateful to be of service in this way. It's my way of giving back, volunteering.

In the end, like everything else, do your homework, trust your guidance and ask Reiki. You can't go wrong!

QUESTIONS TO PONDER
CHECKLIST

☐ How do you see yourself starting? Meditate on where and when and put it out there. Ask Reiki and listen to the answer.

☐ Think of ways to educate people in your community about Reiki. Is there somewhere you can do Reiki samplers or give a talk? This is a great way to get yourself out there, educate people about Reiki and possibly start your business.

☐ Will you set up an LLC? Be a sole proprietor? Do your research and see what works best for you and your business.

☐ Do you have a business plan? A clue? What is your style? You need some sort of foundation, so begin laying it in a way that works for *you.* What do you want? How do you see your business? What does it feel like? How are you inspired to begin? Some ways to help you do this:
—Read as much as you can about creating a business
—Attend classes and educate yourself
—Write down your thoughts
—Create a vision board
—Use affirmations

☐ If you are practicing, you need insurance. Check out IARP.com or Reiki.org for rates.

☐ Are you aware of your intuition? How do you discern it? See? Hear? Know? Smell? Everyone is different. Start paying attention to how you receive your messages.

☐ How will you market yourself? Create at least one of the below and begin passing them out to your friends, your family, and in the community!
—Business Cards
—Rack Cards
—Postcards
—Brochures
—Flyers

☐ Put yourself out there! Join your local Chamber of Commerce and other networking groups so you can grow your business. Start small if this scares you. See what is available in your community and do it!

☐ Get online!
—Create a website
—Get on social media
—Facebook business page
—LinkedIn
—Twitter
—Instagram

☐ Explore professional organizations you can join.
—Better Business Bureau
—National Certification Board for Therapeutic Massage and Bodywork (NCBTMB)
—Chamber of Commerce
—International Association of Reiki Professionals (IARP)
—Reiki Membership Association
—Local networking groups

☐ How will do you deal with the issue of money in your practice? What are your triggers? How do you feel about money and pricing for your services?

☐ Take this a step further. Do your research in this area and set your prices.
—What will you charge for a session?
—What will you charge for your classes?
—How do you feel about it all?

☐ Whether you do it yourself or hire someone, make sure you have an accounting system for your practice.

The Client Side

L et's talk about clients: how to keep them, your relationship with them, how to conduct a session, advance bookings and boundaries. I will share with you some different types of client experiences I've had and also talk about the things I did that worked, as well as some of the things that did not. I hope you find it useful.

Our clients are our bread and butter but they are so much more than that. They are also highly polished mirrors that reflect back to us what we need to learn. (I will repeat this many times over—it's so important!) Over the years, my clients have taught me so much and helped me to heal so many things. I have a client who likes to say we have a collaborative relationship and how right she is. The longer I practice, the more I see the many different ways we all help one another.

When I first wrote this part of the book, I detailed a lot of client experiences I have had over the years. I have since edited that portion, as what I had written seemed mean-spirited and judgmental. I talked so much about the "high-maintenance clients" that it was obvious I still had some work to do in that area. This is what I mean by highly polished mirrors reflecting back to us what we need to see. It seems some were more highly polished than others!

I now am ready to give thanks for those blessings and receive the healing they were there to give me. I've decided not to go into detail, but instead, will speak in more general terms about the types of things you may encounter with your clients and/or students.

The Client Side

Because Reiki gives us what we need when we need it, everyone will have a different type of client experience. My high-maintenance gal might be your dream client. I think we should be grateful for each and every one of our clients.

Once You Have Them, How Do You Keep Them?

I've shared with you how to find your clients and now I'd like to talk about how to keep them. What can you do to ensure they have a good experience and keep coming back? If you plan on making a living doing Reiki, this is important. I believe most people can be talked into coming that first time. Many are curious about Reiki but what makes them want to return to you? What sets you apart from all of the other Reiki professionals?

Respect and Communication

A healthy relationship has at its core *respect* and *good communication*. If you have those two things, you cannot go wrong. I'd like to add to those *speaking your truth* and *coming from your heart* as well. A recipe for success! This might sound corny but it's true and very simple. Love yourself, love your clients, treat everyone with respect, be kind, and keep those lines of communication open.

There are so many different reasons people come for Reiki. Some have heard about it and are curious, some are led intuitively and don't really know why they are there, but just know they need to be there, some are trying a new practitioner. They are all coming to receive Reiki from *you,* so please be there for them. One-hundred percent. They deserve your time and attention. Listen to them when they speak. Make eye contact. Don't talk about yourself unless it's to tell them about the session or if they ask a question. This is their time.

Be on Time

First things first, be on time. Don't make your clients wait. I believe it is disrespectful to them. Of course, sometimes tardiness can't be helped, but as a general rule, plan your day accordingly so you are fresh and ready to go for your clients. If you have a full day of Reiki planned, give yourself enough time between sessions.

I block out my appointments every two hours. That gives me plenty of time with each client, including time to change the sheets, refresh the room, check messages, go the bathroom, and eat or drink something. I am relaxed and ready to go for each new client. I never want to have an assembly line, rushing to each next person. Clients can feel that energy and it is not a good way to start the session.

Be Professional

You are beginning a new relationship with this person. Even if it is someone you know, consider it a new relationship, because it is. That person is coming to you for assistance, for healing. Treat the session as such and respect it. With your friends or family, you are also creating a new relationship. Allow them to see you in this new role.

Consider your language, your clothing, your space. You want everything to say "successful Reiki Master." Do you project this? When I first started my practice, I wore sweats and went barefoot; it was so great not to be in corporate America anymore! After a while, I realized I was projecting a sloppy image and cleaned up my act.

Ask yourself how you wish to be seen and perceived, and dress accordingly.

The Client Side

Preparing the Space

Before you start your day of seeing clients or teaching a class, you may want to clear and set sacred space. Do it first thing, at the beginning of your work shift, with the intention of it being for all of the clients and lasting the entire day. Do it the day of your classes, before the students arrive. When working with clients, I do a smaller prayer of intention before I begin to work on them, but the majority of the work is done at the beginning of the day.

Clear the room, using the power symbol (CKR). Draw it to the four directions, to the heavens and to the earth, and then draw all the Reiki symbols in the middle of the room. This clears the room and sets sacred space.

Next, "strengthen your light," which involves drawing a large power symbol (CKR), in front of yourself and beaming it into you. Then draw a smaller one at each chakra, beginning at the root and saying CKR ending at the crown, guiding the symbols into your body, saying CKR three times. Next, draw the two power symbols, the CKR and the Usui DKM on your hands.

If you are so inclined, your prayer of intention comes next. When I say mine, I name all of my clients and myself, asking that all our guides, angels, archangels, beings of light, teachers (seen and unseen), Reiki Masters, etc. join us in the healing. I state that I know that Reiki flows through me and not from me. I ask that my ego and personality step aside and that I not be concerned with outcome or expectation.

I ask that anything less than 100 percent pure light leave the space and stay gone. I give gratitude and thanks for Reiki, the places I practice, the people I practice with, my teachers, clients and students, and for the ability to channel Reiki. If there is anything else I am guided to say I add that as well.

You can create your own prayer of intention. This is an example of what I've developed over the years. I've pieced it together after hearing it from various teachers and Reiki colleagues.

Please understand you do not need to do any of the above—Reiki will flow just fine without it, but I like to have a protocol. I feel it gives Reiki respect and I just love to do it.

The First Session with Your Client

So what exactly do you do when a client comes to see you for the first time? You've spent all that time marketing and networking and here the client is! Have you given any thought to what you'll actually do?

It can be scary if you are not prepared, so I will now share with you what I do, give you some ideas, and then you can develop your own style. Use my suggestions to help you find *your* way.

Make it easy on yourself and take your ego out of it. Sometimes clients are nervous when they come for a session,, so don't take anything personally and don't try to be the clients' best friend—just be the best Reiki Master you can be. Everything will fall into place, I promise.

A mantra I use in my teaching and one I've adopted with clients that is very useful is "meet them where they are." Every client will be different; learn to go with the flow. It helps if you are organized, on time and ready.

Important: we are our own healers. The person you are working on is doing his or her own healing. You are a channel, an instrument. You are providing the sacred space and helping your clients to facilitate their own healing. You are not doing the healing. Remember this. It should take some pressure off of you.

Each new client of mine gets a brochure, a business card, and a promotional pen with my contact information. Sometimes I have the new client choose a crystal. I like the idea of having my clients take away something to remember their session.

I also have new clients fill out a Client Information Form. The one I use comes from the *Reiki, The Healing Touch: First and Second Degree Manual* by William Rand. It's a basic consent form and it will also give you your client's contact information. Put that information in a database for future marketing opportunities (mailing, cards, etc.) and mail each new client a thank you card within a week of his or her appointment. Yes, a thank you card. Not an email or a text—but a hand-written thank you card in the mail. You are grateful, aren't you?

Next ask new clients what brought them to you. Why Reiki? How did they find you? (The answer will help you know which marketing tools are working.) Explain to them what Reiki is and how it works. Let them know that everyone's experience is different but give them a general idea. You can walk them though a "typical" Reiki session so they know what to expect when they lie down on the table.

I find that this initial talk time helps to relax new clients and alleviate any fear or apprehension they may have come in with. It also gives their healing intention time to bubble up. I find even if they are not aware of it, folks come in with some sort of healing intention and it almost always surfaces during this early talk time. You also want to give them time to get used to your energy and feel comfortable. This initial talk time takes about 15 minutes or so. There are some people who want to get right down to business and lie on the table, without any talk time. Take your lead from your clients and respect what they need. Remember to meet them where they are.

Before they lie down on the table, ask them if they need to go to the bathroom or if they'd like any water. I always make sure that I have water in the room just in case. Sometimes the throat chakra acts up during a session and clients begin to cough, so I also have cough drops close by. Blankets are nearby in case they get cold. I play healing Reiki music and ask them if the volume is ok or if they need it adjusted.

I tell them I don't talk while they are on the table, but if they need something not to hesitate to ask. I also tell them if they need to talk I'll let them drive that. Most people like to go off into their own journey but I have a handful of clients who like to talk during their sessions. This used to bother me, but I've come to realize it's what they need. Some are lonely and others have no one to talk to. It serves its purpose.

Remember, Reiki gives us what we need when we need it. Trust that it knows what it is doing. *You* are not directing the session.

On the Table

Right before the session begins, I like to ask clients to set an intention. I tell them it can be more than one and it can be mental, emotional, physical and/or spiritual, that Reiki works on all of these levels simultaneously and intuitively. I then share an affirmation I developed as not everyone understands what an intention is or has one.

It goes like this: *I am ready and willing to let go of those things that no longer serve me or my highest good so I may bring in those things that do.*

I believe this really is the essence of Reiki; it gets rid of those energies that do not serve us and allows us to bring in more light. Next, I tell clients I am stepping out of the room to go wash my hands. This allows them to acclimate to the room and get more comfortable.

We get started when I return and I trust that the Reiki will guide us and give us both what we need when we need it. It's really as easy as putting your hands on the person and getting out of the way. Remember, Reiki flows through us, not from us.

I practice on the client for about an hour, give or take. I like to do the prescribed hand positions, however, I do veer off in another direction if I am guided to do so. I also use the symbols during a session.

I work with a number of different symbols, both Usui and Karuna. I'm never really sure how many or which ones I am going to use. I wait for them to appear. This is something I've always felt comfortable with and trust that the symbols will appear when they are needed. I sometimes draw them on the client or say them in my head or use my breath to blow them into the area that needs healing. I listen to my guidance.

In my practice, I like to begin with the head, to make a connection, and end with the feet, to ground the client. At the end of the session, I tell clients I am done and leave the room for a few minutes to give them time to come back into their body and sit up if they are ready. I wash my hands, do the dry bathing technique to get rid of any excess energy, and come back into the room.

When I return, we sit down again to talk a bit. I offer clients a piece of dark chocolate and some water. Then I tell them it's important to stay hydrated after a session. You also want to make sure your clients are grounded before they leave (thus the chocolate).

I will then ask them if there is anything they would like to share about their session. Some folks do and some don't. At this point, if it is appropriate, I will share with them any messages or impressions I might have received. While I don't consider myself a psychic, I sometimes receive messages and see/hear/know things when I am doing a Reiki session. I always use discernment when sharing.

When I do share, if someone asks me "what does that mean?" I always give that question back to them. It really doesn't matter what I think it means. It's their interpretation that is important. This is also a good way for your clients to tap into their own intuition.

Just like sharing information with a client, be careful not to diagnose your client. We are not medical professionals. Occasionally, I have asked folks questions about their health and guided them to see a doctor when appropriate, but you really have to be careful here. Use discernment.

This step-by-step information may be obvious and you may wonder why I put it in with so much detail. I did because I am asked these questions quite a bit by those students of mine who are getting ready to begin a practice. And while I don't expect you to do exactly as I say, I feel it will give you some ideas that you can build upon.

Over the years, my clients seemed to like this approach. I also think it's one of the reasons my practice has been so successful. I treat my clients with kindness and respect, make them feel special (they are!), give them time, and listen. It has been my experience that people want and need to be heard.

Booking the Next Appointment

When you finish up a session with clients, always ask them to book their next appointment. It ensures they make another appointment and that they are able to get the time and day they desire. This is preferable to them waiting until they feel they need another session and not being able to get in for a while. I recommend that if they have the time and the money to get Reiki every four to six weeks, and more if they are so guided.

At this time I also encourage them to purchase a three-pack. This is paid up front for three future appointments, giving them a $10 discount off each individual session. Many of my clients booked all three appointments at once. Most came monthly. They got in the habit of doing this and many of them did it for years and years.

Scheduling subsequent appointments is a good way to teach your clients the importance of monthly Reiki sessions. It fills your calendar, puts the money in the bank up front, and helps to create a successful Reiki practice.

Thank-You Cards

I highly encourage you to send thank-you notes to your clients after their first session. It's important to acknowledge them and express gratitude. I received a thank-you card after my first Reiki session and it made me feel special and loved. I wanted to pass that on to my clients so I started this practice.

I also send thank-you cards to my students after a class and encourage you to do so. This little act goes such a long way. Treat your clients as you wish to be treated.

Setting Your Schedule

When do you want to work? When are your clients available? Decide which days you want to work and set up a schedule for yourself. That way, you won't have appointments all over the place. Because my husband worked a lot of hours and we don't have any children, I could pretty much work whenever I wanted. I chose to make myself available on nights and weekends, because many of my clients worked a Monday-Friday, nine-to-five schedule.

I worked every other weekend, some days and some nights, alternating early and late starts to accommodate the schedule of my clients. I tried to make my schedule as diverse as possible and still have time for a life. It really helped to have my hours mapped out in advance so when people called, I could easily offer them dates and times.

Also think about how many clients you want to see in a day and week. Find the number that works for you. Everyone is different. How many sessions do you want in a week? What's your magic number?

When I first started my Reiki practice, my schedule was all over the place as I didn't have very strong boundaries in this area. I had to learn the hard way. It wasn't until I got tired of working all the time and feeling resentful that I created a consistent schedule. I was my own worst enemy in the beginning. I would be so afraid of not giving clients a time/date they wanted. I worried that they would go to someone else, or be upset with me. I always try to accommodate the client, but if they want a time I can't do, I am no longer afraid to offer them an alternate time. Most people are happy to work with you. Don't be afraid to ask for what you need.

Call To Confirm

It's a good idea to call and confirm your client's appointments. Trust me, it will save you time and money. I would make my calls for the week on Sunday evening and it took all of 15 minutes, if that.

Many times when I called, appointments would need to be changed. Because I was confirming sessions ahead of time, it was easy and I could adjust my schedule as necessary.

You don't want to have to do this the day of, or worse yet, deal with a no-show or last-minute cancellation. In all the years I've had my practice, I can count on one hand the number of no-shows I've experienced and have also had very few last-minute cancellations. Since the majority of my clientele are older, they prefer a phone call to a text message. Remember, meet your clients where they are, but do be sure to contact them.

Calling In Sick

It's okay to call in sick. Sometimes things prevent us from showing up to work: illness, family emergencies, death, sick loved ones or pets. Please know it is okay to reschedule, as you are not expected to do it all. Soldiering through does not make you noble.

Take time outs when you need them. You'll be better off for it. How can you help your clients with their healing if you are not taking care of yourself first? I think we put more pressure on ourselves in this area than our clients. Take guilt and fear out of the equation and give yourself a break.

The Relationship Between You and Your Client

In the beginning, I wanted all of my clients to like me. I mean I was desperate to have them like me. This is so embarrassing for me to admit but it's true. It really showed up when I taught classes, but it popped into my practice as well. This is something I've struggled with all of my life and something Reiki is helping me to heal.

As long as I followed the guidance of "respect and communication," I was fine. If my ego and personality got in the way, the trouble began. I took so much personally!

Let me save you the time and heartache—don't do this! Know your triggers, watch for them, and ask Reiki to help you to heal them. Try to be the observer, not the reactor.

Remember, you represent your business. You want to provide a safe haven for your clients. Yes, Reiki is bringing up your stuff, and yes, your clients are highly polished mirrors, so if you do behave badly, use it as a teaching example.

Walk your talk as best you can. Sometimes this is easier said than done, so ask Reiki to help you.

Be Who You Are

And please, be yourself! Don't be afraid to let people see the real you. Energy doesn't lie. If you are trying to be some version of "the perfect Reiki Master," it won't work. Trust me. I've seen this and I've done this and it's not pretty.

When I first started on this path, I thought I had to be like the guru on the mountain. I was afraid to be who I really was. I thought I wasn't "spiritual" enough, that I was too silly or too naughty or too something wrong. I never really felt that I measured up to the lofty goal of Reiki Master, thus my fear.

Fortunately, I got over that pretty quickly. I discovered that the more I allowed me to be who I really was, the more relaxed the client would be. What a relief! I did not have to "act as if" or pretend to be a know it all Reiki Master. I was me, with the Reiki inside. I asked Reiki to help me to be more comfortable in my own skin, in this new role as Reiki Master. And Reiki always gives us what we need if it is for our best and highest good.

When we allow others to see us, to really see us, we connect with them on a very deep level. Let your clients get to know you, the real you.

To Friend or Not to Friend

Again, I want to stress how important it is to have a professional relationship with your clients. They are coming to you for a service and you are providing that service to the best of your abilities. You are treating them with respect and communicating with them on a deep and loving level. Reiki sessions are so intimate and we really get to know our clients. Sometimes because of this, they confuse that feeling with friendship and want to take the friendship outside of the Reiki room.

Be careful here. Tread lightly. I'm not saying it can't be done or that I've never done it with success, but you really do need to use discernment here. Speaking from my own experience, I've confused what I've gotten from the Reiki energy with the person giving it to me. I practically stalked one of my teachers, wanting her to like me and be my friend. It was so embarrassing.

It wasn't until I began experiencing it myself that I realized what was happening. We feel so good from a Reiki session or a class and we can transfer that feeling onto the person who is giving it. We want more of this feeling so it makes sense that we want to be with that person. It's only now, so many years later, that I am learning how to navigate those waters with any sort of grace.

Set your boundaries and don't try to be anyone's best friend. Do be the best Reiki Master you can be. Be friendly with your clients, treat them with respect, communicate, come from your heart, and be yourself. But don't forget to set boundaries.

Client Experiences

Mirror, Mirror

I've spoken at length about clients being highly polished mirrors who have much to teach us. And they do! I can't stress this enough. Be prepared! There are so many facets to running your Reiki business. Business practices are as important as the mental and emotional challenges you will encounter.

Your issues are bound to come up, many times in the guise of clients. Know this! If you can keep this level of awareness, you can see the opportunity for healing that is presented. Remember, everyone and everything is your teacher, especially your clients.

Some things I've learned from my clients:

- Not everyone is going to like me or Reiki
- I might not like all of my clients
- Some clients may need more than Reiki; you can't help them (you can refer them)
- How to set and keep boundaries
- When to let a client go
- Being honest and using discernment

I think it's very important to discern the difference between your issues and the issues of your students and clients. Reiki is not only bringing up your stuff, but your client's as well. Be conscious of what is happening and don't be afraid of standing in your power if need be. That collaborative relationship? The longer I practice, the more I realize how true this is.

Below are a few examples of clients I have had and in some cases, some of the challenges I've had with them. Every single one of them taught me something and I am so grateful. I notice as I grow in my practice, so do my thoughts on my clients. In the beginning, I was more judgmental, critical, and even blaming. My clients have helped me to heal many things and I have softened in my relationships as a result.

You will be graced with so much healing for yourself and others. Allow the relationship to unfold and be a willing participant. Remember that it is a collaborative relationship. It's not so much about me serving them, as us working together, learning from each other, and ultimately, moving toward unconditional love and acceptance. Clients have as much teaching and healing for you as you have for them. Be willing to accept it, and don't resist it.

I love new Reiki clients! I love watching the light bulb moments, the "aha" moments, the energy leading them to new ideas, people, places and things that help them make the changes they need to make. In its purest form, this is how Reiki works.

These clients allow the light in and they go with the flow. They trust. And they keep coming back. They are passionate and enthusiastic and know that even though the road might get a little bumpy or rough, it all works out for their best and highest good.

I am grateful and lucky that this is the majority of my clients. Perhaps again because I was/am this client/student. I don't know. I'm just happy to be of service. I want clients who want Reiki. I want clients who look forward to their sessions and are open to whatever those sessions bring.

I have clients who bring notebooks to their sessions and write down what bubbles up for them. I love this dedication to Reiki!

Over the years, they have a history of their growth. I love the clients who want to talk about their sessions and what those mean. If I am guided, I will share with them what came up for me, when it is appropriate. Now, for those examples:

Not Everyone is Going to Like You or Reiki

This would be the "Gift Certificate" client. I have sold a lot of gift certificates and for the most part, I wish I hadn't. In one way, offering these felt like stealing. Most of the people who received the certificates never showed up. The giver had good intentions, but the receiver did not want or believe in Reiki.

I felt badly for those who did show up. Mostly they were husbands or family members the giver of the certificate was trying to help. Reiki had been such a healing tool for them, they wanted to share it. But here's the thing I've discovered from these folks—they were not guided to come. They were told to come. They didn't believe in Reiki. I told them to give it a chance, and at the very least, it will be a nice hour of rest.

With the exception of a few, most did not return. Unless it's for someone who is already getting Reiki and loves it, it's not such a good idea, based on my experience. I never took it personally if these folks told me they didn't like it or didn't feel anything, which happened on occasion.

You Might Not Like All Your Clients

Which brings up something that also took me a long time to accept and become comfortable with: it's okay to not like some clients. It's okay to not accept someone or keep someone as a client if you don't like his or her vibe. For some reason, I thought I had to like everyone and take everyone on as a client.

Client Experiences

Why? It's that "peace and love" mentality I had. If I was a "good" Reiki Master, then I'd be able to love and accept everyone. On some level that is true, but not in the way I'm talking about.

Trust your gut and follow through. Don't do anything you don't feel comfortable doing. You will be able to discern which clients can help you with your healing and which ones you are not supposed to work with. If you are unsure, ask Reiki to help you.

I am ashamed to say that I had a few clients I referred to as "high maintenance." These were the ones who drove me crazy: those who constantly came late, or forgot their payment, or had the habit of canceling at the last minute or worse yet, being no shows. I am lucky I didn't have too many of these, but I did have a few.

At this point in my journey, I see these clients as blessings. I'm not going to provide any details about them, but would like to take this opportunity to share a shift I experienced.

I had one particular client for about five years. I saw her once a month without fail. To be honest, I didn't always look forward to her sessions. I had a hard time relating to her and the things she talked about. And she liked to talk! Her sessions often ran over, and it was difficult to get her both on and off the table. She did enjoy the Reiki and said she noticed the effect it had on her life. I was happy for this, yet there were still times I flinched when I saw her name in my datebook.

Then something changed. One night, after a session, she was walking out to her car and as I watched her, I felt such a surge of love for her. I realized how much she had helped me to transcend my judgment and fear and I felt so grateful for her. I no longer thought of her as high maintenance and began looking at all of my clients in a new light.

When to Let a Client Go

There have been a few times I've had to let a client go. It wasn't easy, but it was necessary. In every case, I waited too long because I was afraid to do it. I was afraid of hurting their feelings or worried about what they might say about me in the community. I was so worried about bad press! So I ignored my intuition and kept seeing them until I just about exploded. I will share just a few examples here. Please trust your gut and listen to your intuition. Had I done this, all of us would have suffered less.

A client was referred to me by a colleague in the clinic where I practiced. Initially, I got a "bad vibe," but because he was a referral I agreed to work with him. From the initial visit on, I was uncomfortable. I sensed he was there not simply for Reiki, but I couldn't put my finger on exactly what. He seemed like a lonely person, and I rationalized that the Reiki would help him. He wanted "therapy" and would talk about deeply personal problems, many of them sexual and inappropriate. I would ask him to stop, tell him I was not a therapist, and offered to refer him to a person better qualified to help him with his issues.

Many times, I explained to him what Reiki was and what I could and could not do for him. In retrospect, I realize I should have cut it off after that initial uncomfortable visit, but those old feelings of fear and insecurity came back and I continued to see him, each visit growing more and more uncomfortable.

One time after a session, we were talking, and he said something extremely inappropriate. I responded with "I can no longer work on you if you speak to me like that." He left. Two weeks later, he had another appointment, and I felt sick to my stomach about seeing him and went home, leaving a note on the door before he came.

Again, two weeks later, he had another scheduled appointment, and I began to feel sick again. When he came in, I told him right away that I was no longer able to work with him. He got mad and yelled. He was very hurt and upset. I was alone with him in the clinic, and I was scared. He was a big guy and very emotional.

However, I stood firm, walked him to the door, and asked him to leave. He did. I was so relieved! This situation never would have gotten to that point if I had trusted my judgment and just felt secure in saying *no*, instead of being drawn into the situation of "trying to please and help everyone." It was a very good lesson and one I don't think I'll repeat any time soon. I'm grateful for it.

Sometimes it is less obvious, but just as important to part ways with a client. You can usually feel it coming and they can, too, even if they (or you) are not consciously aware of it. There is a feeling of being done, of the client not getting anything from the session. I've had this happen a few times.

One woman had been coming to me for a few years, continuously buying session three-packs. She was in a transitional point in her life when I met her and it seemed that Reiki was working to help her find her way. After a while, though, something changed; the energy felt flat, but she kept coming back. She appeared unhappy and complained a lot. I made the mistake of trying to placate her, instead of just allowing her to talk. Inside, I was frustrated, not understanding why she kept coming, or why I couldn't help her, yet I didn't talk to her about this. I kept trying to solve her problems. My ego was quite engaged. This went on for a few sessions, with the tension growing and both of us becoming more frustrated.

Finally, she told me that she felt Reiki wasn't doing her any good. And even though I agreed with her, I took it personally. Of course, I didn't let on, but I was upset. We talked a bit and I told her perhaps it was time to go. She was concerned because she had paid in advance for her sessions, and didn't want to lose the money. I told her I'd refund her money. She was relieved and we parted ways.

Like I said, I took this personally, like I had somehow failed her. It was a good lesson for me. A few years later, I ran into her and she took a Reiki class from me. It was good to see her and to see that she had moved on and was thriving. I was happy for her and I'm grateful to her for the lessons she offered me.

How to Set and Keep Boundaries

There are also times when we need to be firm in setting and holding boundaries. This is an area I needed a lot of work in and I received many opportunities! After a while, I became sick of feeling frustrated or angry and allowed myself to ask for what I needed from the clients. At first, I was nervous or scared that I'd hurt their feelings, make them angry, or that they'd never come back, until I realized that they were doing that to me and why did I want a client who didn't respect me? Why was I reinforcing this bad behavior?

What I am referring to are certain things I found unacceptable. For example:

- The client who forgot his money at every session. This became a repeated habit and even though I'd remind him when I confirmed, he continued to forget. It got to the point I had to send him a bill and then follow up with that. Had he been honest with me and told me he needed the session, but didn't have the money, I would have worked something out. I finally had to tell him if he didn't pay up front, he couldn't have a session. However, it took me a long time to be able to say this. This "healing experience" for me spoke to my money and self-esteem (deserving) issues.

- The client who was always late. Every single appointment, she would be at least 20 minutes late. She'd rush in in a frenzy, and then spend another 10 minutes or so apologizing and telling me why she was late. In the beginning, I just ran late because I was too afraid to say anything. Sound familiar?

  The pattern kept repeating itself in different scenarios until I got it right. Finally, after one more late arrival, I cut short her time on the table. It wasn't fair to the people after her to have to wait and I was tired of it. Once, when she got off the table, she told me "This session was a complete waste of my time." I suggested that maybe Reiki wasn't the tool for her and she agreed. I never saw her again.

- Being honest and using discernment. This can get tricky and you really need to do an honest self-assessment here. Is your client mirroring something back to you that needs healing or is he or she being disrespectful and rude? I've been on both sides of this equation and It's not an easy one.

  I tend to err on the side of caution and give a client a lot of leeway but sometimes I've come to the conclusion that it's not me, it's the client. When this happens, you need to have an honest conversation with yourself and your client. There have been times I was not able to fire a client face to face so I wrote the person a letter. I was as honest as I could be, while still being kind and respectful. I'm lucky this has only happened twice in 10 years, but it can happen so be prepared.

I think you get the idea. In all of the above examples, I can see how each brought me some healing. I needed to learn these things as my business grew to be successful, both personally and professionally. I learned how to set boundaries, to speak my truth with kindness and compassion, and to stand in my power—all things that I sorely lacked. I'm so grateful to Reiki and to my clients for everything it and they have taught me. The learning continues to this day.

Reiki Stories

There are so many interesting Reiki stories to tell. So many! Because Reiki works on many levels and it gives us what we need when we need it, there can be many different types of healing and outcomes.

Most people enjoy an hour of rest and relaxation. A Reiki session can feel like a very deep meditation. You aren't exactly asleep and you aren't exactly awake. You're in that floaty place of no thought. Afterwards you feel as if you took a very restful nap.

Then there is the twitchy type of session, which is a not really a favorite of the person on the table. From a practitioner's viewpoint, I think all that twitching and jerking are signs of energy moving. My brother, for example, jerks around so much on the table, I have to be careful to stay back, lest I get kicked or hit. He releases a lot of big energy.

People sleep, snore, cry, laugh, and talk during a session. I never know what to expect and I think that's why I like doing Reiki so much. Every day is different and every session is different. Even the same people have different sessions. It is never the same. I love that. I can honestly say in all the years I've been doing Reiki, I've never been bored. I look forward to each and every session and I know that in those sessions, clients are getting exactly what they need, whether they realize it or not. Reiki always works on some level and it does no harm. I love that.

My favorite type of session to give is the kind where both you and your client are completely open and you make a deep connection with the person. It feels as if the two of you are one. It's hard to know where you end and the person begins. I can go so deep when I come out of it, I don't know where I am. I feel that I too have gotten a session.

There are as many types of session experiences as there are clients. Be open to them all. Each one has something to teach us. Now let me share a few Reiki stories.

The Reiki Baby

I love working on children. I haven't worked on many, but the times I did were magical. I have one I always think of as my Reiki baby. I met her before she was born; I could feel her vibration deep in her mother's womb. I gave her a treatment a few weeks after she was born and continued to work on her every so often, until I moved.

Her mother had been receiving Reiki from me for about a year. One day, as I was working on her stomach, I had a vision of her with a new baby girl. I didn't know that she was trying to conceive. I knew she was not yet pregnant, but felt very soon she would be. We talked a little about this after her session. She told me she and her husband were trying to have a baby.

A few weeks later, she called to tell me she was pregnant. She continued to come for sessions every few months and these sessions were nothing short of magical. I could feel the baby in a way I never have with other pregnant women. It felt as if we were communicating on some level. If the baby had been moving or kicking or active, when I'd put my hands on Mom's stomach, she would get very quiet. I swear I could hear her purring. I knew this baby loved Reiki.

A few days before this baby was born, I worked on her mom again. During the session, I saw myself working on the two of them, with the baby lying on her mother's stomach, and my hands on both of them. After the session, I told my client this, and she said she had a similar vision. She asked if I'd come to her home after the baby was born, and I happily agreed.

The day I came to her home, the baby was four weeks old. I started by working on her mom a bit and then we put the baby on her mom's stomach. Again, I felt that deep connection with this special Reiki baby. She had the most joyous smile on her face and lay still for a very long time. We stayed this way until her older brother woke up from a nap and came into the room. He walked over to the couch and nestled in beside his mom.

I arranged my hands so I was touching all three of them, and we sat this way for a very long time. It was early winter and the sun was streaming in from the windows. It felt thick and lazy and also energized by the Reiki at the same time. It was as if we were in this magic bubble of joy. Soon the family dog wandered over and settled in against my legs—one big, happy Reiki family.

After a bit, the session ended and Mom and I sat and talked about the experience. In that moment, I truly understood the phrase "all are one." That is exactly how it felt. The baby took a nap in her swing and her older brother curled up on the couch with his blanket. His mom lay next to him, relaxed and happy. I left, thinking how lucky I am to be able to practice Reiki for a living. These types of experiences are so special, and I am so grateful to be of service and to have such intimate connections in my work. This is my job!

The Cowboy

When I worked at the cancer center, there was a period of time where I worked on a lot of older men. This was a new demographic for me and I am grateful to have treated this population. Those men taught me a lot.

One experience in particular comes to mind and it really illustrates the healing powers of Reiki. An older man with an advanced case of lung cancer came for a session. A tough, old, cowboy type, he was there because his wife suggested it; having Reiki had not been his idea. He was reluctant to initially lie on the table and he wasn't shy about voicing it, but he was a good sport and came to the session. He told me he didn't believe it was going to work for him, that his wife made him do it.

I explained to him what he could expect during the session and got him arranged on the table, careful to make room for his oxygen tank. He seemed agitated and nervous and I learned he also had a significant hearing loss.

The session started and he relaxed immediately. He went in and out of sleep during his time on the table and it felt as if his body was just soaking up the Reiki. Afterwards, I helped him to sit up and asked him how he felt. He told me he could hear much clearer! This shocked him and he leaned over and gave me a big hug! He told me he felt great and tears came to his eyes.

He received Reiki weekly for the remainder of his radiation treatments. His wife took a Reiki Level One class so she could work on him at home. I lost touch with them and often wondered how they were.

A few weeks ago, I ran into his wife at the grocery store and she told me that her husband was cancer free! She continues to do Reiki on him and we both believe that Reiki played a significant role in helping to heal him.

Using Discernment

Previously I talked about not diagnosing your clients, and using discernment when you get a sense that something is wrong. What follows is an example of a time when I suggested that a client see her doctor.

I used to work on a friend once a month and one night, while I was working on her, I felt something amiss in her pelvic region. I heard "something is growing." After the session, I asked her if she was experiencing anything in that area and she told me she thought she might be pregnant. She said that her period had been late for a few months and she felt "weird" in that area.

She took a pregnancy test and it came out negative. I worked on her the next month and this time it felt even stronger and again I heard "something is growing." This time, I *knew* it was not a baby, but possibly a tumor. After the session, I told her it might be a good idea to see her doctor as I felt some discordant energy in that area.

Since she still hadn't had her period, but knew she wasn't pregnant, she decided to do so. She went to the doctor and found out she indeed did have a tumor. It was benign, and she had it removed, along with a hysterectomy.

Should I have said something? I think so. If my client had not been a friend, I might have acted differently, but maybe not. Again, I think this is a case-by-case judgment call and you need to trust your gut. It's important to use discernment with all of your clients.

The Cancer Patient

When I first began my practice, I thought I'd volunteer to do Reiki with women and children. I had a hard time finding a good fit and growing frustrated one day, I sat down in my center and did a meditation on it. My very next client became my volunteer opportunity and one that continues to this day.

A young woman came to me with a gift certificate for a session. Her aunt had given it to her, as she could not afford a session. She had breast cancer, had just finished chemo, and was getting ready for radiation treatments. She was the first really sick person I'd ever worked on and if I'm truthful, it really scared me. I remember her taking off her baseball cap and the wig attached to it came off as well. Her head was bald and shiny and at first I was afraid to touch it. I'm grateful to Reiki, for it helped me to overcome this fear.

While I was working on her, I "heard" that she was to be my volunteer opportunity, that I would be working one on one with women who had cancer, offering them free sessions while they went through treatment. I liked this message! I felt it would be more beneficial for me to work one on one with someone as opposed to a group Reiki Share, which was what I'd been considering.

I worked with this first patient weekly, then monthly, for years. It opened the door for others and at any given time, I was seeing four or five cancer patients a month, free of charge. This went on until I moved to Arizona, where I was then offered the opportunity to start a Reiki program at the cancer center. It was a perfect fit, as I was very comfortable and had experience working with this population.

One thing I didn't mention was that when I offered that first woman free sessions, she told me that while she was on the table, she had prayed to find a way to continue these sessions. I believe I heard her prayer.

I worked on the woman for a few years and watched her as she healed her cancer, went back to school, got a new job in her field, and bought a home. Another example of Reiki's healing powers.

My Own Healing Experience

Now I'd like to share a Reiki healing I experienced. In February of 2009, I travelled to Sedona for a retreat type of vacation. I needed some time away from work, some alone time, and was in great need of a healing session. The previous July, my sister-in-law had been killed by a hit-and-run drunk driver; this event sent me into a tailspin of grief. I had been stuffing my feelings and emotions and they manifested in deep physical and emotional pain.

I made an appointment with my teacher for a Reiki session. I felt self-conscious as I lay down, hyper-aware of everything in the room. I worried that the healing wouldn't take, that I was permanently broken, that maybe even she could not help me. I felt hopeless.

She had been working on me for about 15 minutes when she got to my heart. Her hands were so cold. She placed them on my heart and then quickly removed them. I heard her moving around and soon a crystal bowl in the tone of the heart chakra lay upon my chest. She began to play and the sound of the bowl singing filled the room, deeply vibrating in my body and everything began to shift.

I felt a pressure building up in my chest and I began to cry. The pressure kept building and I kept crying until I was sobbing, then wailing. Snot was pouring out of my nose and I could barely catch my breath. Everything that had been inside of me was finally coming out. It was the biggest release I've ever experienced. I cried and cried until there was nothing left. It felt like hours, but was probably more like 20 minutes. It was amazing.

I felt very safe with my teacher, so I was able to let go. I didn't care what she thought or that others outside of the room could hear me. My need to release was greater than my fear of what other's thought. I blew like a top!

Afterwards, I felt drained and tired, yet lighter than I had in a year. The pain in my neck and shoulders was beginning to subside and my body didn't hurt. The combination of the Reiki, my teacher's energy, the crystal bowl, the vibration of the table, and the lighted Vogel crystals was the alchemy needed to crack the code of my pain and suffering. It was the beginning of my healing.

I tell you this because we, as practitioners, do not know why people come to us, what they have been through, or where they are in their healing. Some might be afraid to let go.

Create a safe space for them and allow them to do the healing they need. Trust your intuition and do what Reiki guides you to do. My teacher "heard" that I needed the bowl. Don't be self-conscious to do what you hear or what your guides are telling you.

I've used breathwork in sessions, chanted the Karuna symbols, and used rattles and drums. I used to worry that it would scare my clients, but I now know that if I'm guided, it's what they need. Give your clients the space and time they need when they are on the table so they can do what they need to do. Meet them where they are. Trust Reiki.

There are so many interesting Reiki stories. Each client and each session is unique. Cherish your clients and your experiences with them. Your life will be richer as a result.

QUESTIONS TO PONDER
CHECKLIST

❒ Respect and communication are the keys to a healthy relationship with your clients. Do you treat others that way? Yourself?

❒ Always speak your truth and come from your heart. Are you able to do this? Does it make you uncomfortable to be who you are, to show people your true self? If so, ask Reiki to help you with healing in this area of your life.

❒ Be professional! This is your job. Dress accordingly, be on time, treat your practice and your clients as you would any other job.

❒ At the start of your day, before seeing clients or teaching a class, don't forget to clear yourself and the room and set sacred space.

❒ Are you friends with your clients? Are you able to separate business from pleasure? Examine how you interact with your clients and what your intentions are.

❒ Set a schedule for yourself and stick to it. List the days of the week and the hours you wish to work. Take time off for yourself.

❒ Don't forget to:
   —Set next appointment at end of session
   —Call to confirm that appointment
   —Send thank-you cards

❒ Trust your instincts with regards to accepting clients or letting them go. Be clear about your intentions. Trust what you feel and don't be afraid to honor your feelings. Set and keep boundaries.

❒ What client experiences have you had? What have they taught you about Reiki? About yourself?

SECTION THREE

We Teach Best What We Most Need to Learn

The Teaching Side

Teaching Reiki is so satisfying and so much fun, although I admit it took a while for me to be able to say that. This is one more area where Reiki can help you to grow and heal. It will bring up your stuff, trust me. I met pretty much all of my boogeymen when I started teaching and I'm grateful for the experiences.

Redefine Teaching

Does the thought of teaching Reiki scare you? If so, you might just need to reframe what teaching means to you, to take away the fear. If you really have no desire to teach, that is fine; just be sure you can discern the difference between fear and no desire. Don't hide!

When I received my Certificate of Completion at my Reiki Master/Teacher class, I told my teacher that I was not going to teach. I took that class because I just wanted to sit in her classroom, get one more attunement, and be in that lovely energy one last time. I had no intention of teaching and never saw myself as a teacher. She replied that I just might be surprised.

I was.

A month to the day after I received that certificate, I had five women in my living room attending a Reiki Level One class. My teaching career was born and it's been going strong ever since. Another thing that same teacher shared with our class was that when people start asking you to teach, it is time for you to teach, whether or not you feel you are ready. (Does anyone ever feel he or she is ready?)

I was smart enough to listen to the guidance that said I was to teach, but I didn't have the confidence. I honestly didn't believe I had what it took to be a teacher. I think the word *teacher* scared me.

One of the few regrets I have in my life is that I never finished college. I went for years and years part-time, but never crafted any of those classes into a degree. I'd stop and start, get distracted, take a year or two off, and then go back. I consider myself a life-long learner and I love being in a classroom, but I never did manage to get that degree.

I've got a lot of life experience that has served me well, but that non-degree status ate away at my self-esteem. How could I teach if I didn't have a degree? Why would anyone listen to what I had to say? To make matters worse, I worked at a college and was constantly reminded of my lack of education by my many degreed co-workers.

Yet this same institution kept asking me to teach Reiki in their Community Education program. Every semester, as they planned their upcoming classes, they'd ask me. Every semester, I'd turn them down. I was only now getting comfortable teaching women I knew in my living room; there was no way I was going to teach strangers in a college! Me? I don't think so!

After a while, I got really sick of myself and my fear and decided that the next time they asked me to teach a Reiki class, I would do it. When they did ask, I said yes and I told them that no matter what I said, do not allow me to go back on my word. I knew I had some wiggle room before the catalog would be printed and I knew I'd probably try to squirm out of it if I could. Twice, I went to them with really good excuses and they would not let me out of my contract. Twice, I cursed myself for telling them I would do it.

The Teaching Side

The classes went well. My fear was just that—fear. I Did It Afraid and discovered it wasn't as bad as my fear had led me to believe. The classes were well attended and I had repeat students for the next level. I also began teaching Vision Board classes that were quite successful. In fact, I really enjoyed the role of teacher and began having fun with it.

The Shift

So what shifted? One day I was talking to a colleague about my fear of teaching. She is someone who had taken one of my classes and told me she thought I was a good teacher. What is funny is that on some level, I owned that. I was well prepared, I knew my material and could make a connection with my students. I was myself and used humor in the classroom. I was able to create a relaxed and enjoyable class, where the students learned at their own pace. I met them where they were, without even knowing it.

So why all the fear? Because I still had that vision of a teacher in my head, someone serious, someone with a degree. Not me! And then it occurred to me to lose that label and just share with people what I love and what I do every day and have been doing every day for years. Share Reiki. Be Reiki. In fact, why not invite Reiki into the classroom and ask *it* to guide the class and allow myself to be a channel for that beautiful life force energy. Why not?

So I did.

It made all the difference in the world. With a shift in my thinking, I completely changed how I felt about teaching; I was sharing what I knew. I did that every day. It was easy. While I didn't feel confident as a teacher, I was confident talking about Reiki. I love to mentor students and share my Reiki stories. Now I would do it in a classroom.

This shift opened the door to so many opportunities! I would teach at this college and another one for two years. I began teaching Reiki, Vision Board, and Writing classes for our local Parks and Recreation department. All of a sudden, I was a teacher. Me!

I invite you to look at how you feel about teaching and what you can do to change your thinking if it scares you. Ask yourself what you are afraid of and then ask Reiki to help you to heal this issue.

As I mentioned in a previous chapter, with all of this teaching came a lot of (free) advertising. My name and class information were displayed in the college catalogs and sent out into the community. It was an excellent way for me to broaden my client base and get my Reiki practice out there. I received many new clients and students and I was finally able to get over my fear of teaching and my feelings of not measuring up.

Fear and Teaching

So many of my students are afraid to start teaching. They really want to get out there and do it, yet they have held themselves back. They have many reasons, but it usually boils down to fear. You just have to do it.

When I began hearing from my students and new teachers, over and over, how afraid they were, I began sharing my story and eventually this book was born. Know that most people are nervous and fearful to begin teaching. Many never take that first step.

So do whatever it is you have to do to make yourself move forward. Whether it is starting your business, teaching, practicing, whatever it is that has you frozen in the headlights, figure out what you can do to snap yourself out of it. You can do it. If I did it, anyone can. Reiki really does heal us. It gives us what we need when we need it, if we are able to just push ahead and Do It Afraid.

The Teaching Side

Below are some questions I am asked by new teachers or those considering teaching Reiki. I think you may be able to relate and hopefully it will help you to get started.

Must You Teach Formally?

Teaching doesn't necessarily mean having a formal class, although that is certainly the most common way to do it. If you are not guided to teach formally, you might want to consider alternative methods of teaching.

I am currently teaching this way. I have a client, an 88-year-old woman whom I met at the cancer center when I worked there. She asked if I would come to her home to work on her and for the last six months or so, I've worked on her most Saturdays. At about the three-month mark, she asked if I'd attune her to Level One. I was delighted to do this, yet I wondered how that would be. Due to her poor health, she wasn't able to attend a day-long class. This provided me with an opportunity to be creative in my teaching.

I brought to her what I would normally give my students— a textbook and folder with handouts. I sat with her a while and explained the basics that I teach in a Reiki Level One class and then gave her the attunement. Her "homework" was to read the book and the material in the handouts. I asked her to make a list of her questions and told her we could discuss them the next time I saw her. If she needed more immediate answers, she could call and/or email me.

This worked and she began reading and practicing. Of course, the only way one really learns Reiki is by doing it so I encouraged her to do the self-Reiki practice. She began a ritual of nightly self-Reiki, and she enjoyed it immensely. She loved that she could sense the energy and feel the heat in her hands. She worked on herself every night for three months straight. It calmed her and helped her to fall asleep and stay asleep, something she had been struggling with for a very long time.

A few months later, she asked me to attune her to Level Two. She felt she was ready and I was happy to accommodate her. She said she could feel Reiki working and believed it was helping her to heal her cancer. Her last scan showed that it had not spread and some of the areas that once showed cancer were now cancer free. She was also noticeably calmer and more at peace. This is the power of Reiki.

Again I brought over all of the materials for Level Two. I introduced her to the Level Two symbols and we spent time with each one, focusing on their meaning and the different ways she could incorporate them into her life. I taught her how to use the distant symbol (HSZSN), to send to her past, present, and future. This is something that really resonated with her, as I hoped it might.

I also gave her a notebook to practice drawing the symbols. I again asked her to write down any questions she might have as she was studying the material and we'd go over them the next time I saw her. And, I encouraged her to continue with the self-healing. I then gave her the Level Two attunement. We will continue to study the levels as long as she needs to. Since I see her weekly, this works out well.

This is an example of how to design a Reiki class to meet the needs of your students. There are many ways to accommodate everyone's needs. (More on this below.) Be creative!

The Teaching Side

Can You Attune People Without a Class?

I remember thinking this when I first was able to pass attunements. I wanted to attune everyone, especially family. After a while, I realized this was not a responsible use of my abilities as a teacher.

That is not to say you can't attune someone without a class as there are creative ways to teach Reiki (as I've described above). However, if you are planning to attune someone, please do so with the intention of teaching that person about Reiki as well. Give "students" a text, materials, sit and talk with them, practice; don't just give them the attunement and be done with it.

We have a responsibility as teachers to educate people about Reiki, along with the attunement.

Scheduling Your Classes

A great piece of advice I got in my Master/Teacher class was to schedule my classes six months out. Get out a calendar and block out how many classes per month you would like to teach. I started out with one day per month. I'd circle the date and save it for a class. That way, when a student asked, "When is your next class?" I could check my calendar and tell them. There was no "I'll get back to you" or "what works for you?" Having a scheduled class is so much more professional.

Scheduling like this sends a signal to the Universe that you are ready. Your students will heed the call and show up. Decide how many days you want to set aside for teaching and set the dates. Are you afraid? That's okay; it's normal to be nervous. Do It Afraid! It's a good way to begin getting over yourself.

Another great piece of advice the same teacher gave me was that when folks start asking you to teach, it's time for you to teach. When I heard this in my Master/Teacher class, I didn't worry, as I figured no one would ask me. Wrong. Upon my return home from my Master/Teacher class, five women asked me to teach, and my first Level One class was born. I didn't feel I was ready, but then again I don't think I ever would have felt I was ready.

I have many students who are being asked to teach and they run from it! They love to talk about it, and I believe this is a way for them to get used to the idea. They are getting ready. And that's fine, but if you can, try not to resist. Your potential students might go elsewhere and then you won't have to be ready. You can stay safe, in your mind, imagining yourself teaching. Stretch yourself instead. Use Reiki to help you. You won't regret it.

How Many Students in a Class?

That is up to you, as there are no rules. What are you comfortable with? Small? Big? Both? I know many Reiki teachers who will not teach a class unless they have a certain number of students. I don't know many who will teach just one. I made a decision early in my teaching career to set the date and teach whoever shows up on that date. I believe we get the people in each class we are supposed to and should go with it. This has always worked for me.

I like small classes and I like big classes. I've taught many classes of one and I've taught many classes of ten. I've taught two classes of 15, with another teacher. All of them were exactly as they were supposed to be. The one-on-one classes are more difficult for me because the lone student tends to be more relaxed and asks more questions. There is also more of a tendency to get off track in a one-on-one class. I was surprised to find the larger classes much easier to teach. It has been my experience that the more students in a class, the quieter it is. Maybe the larger numbers inhibit students from sharing.

The Teaching Side

My favorite size is four to six students and most of my classes tend to be that size. But I'm happy to teach big or little. I also offer private classes and charge a bit more for those.

As a student, I've been in really big classes (25) and smaller ones (3) and I have to say that again each class was exactly how it was supposed to be.

Some of my best classes are the ones where there are husbands and wives, sisters, mothers and daughters, friends, and co-workers; people that come together to learn. These are very special classes. I have a teacher who says we do things not for the reason we think and I see this with those types of classes.

Reiki is so intimate and we learn so much about one another in a class. My husband and I have taken a few classes together and some of our most vulnerable moments happened in those classes. While it was painful at the time, it opened up new layers of our relationship for us to grow into. I see this with other couples as well.

Be Aware

Sometimes a class can really bring up our students' stuff and as teachers, we need to be sensitive and discerning when this happens. It can be like walking a tightrope. You don't want to stop something from happening, so do allow it, but be careful not to let it become a private therapy session for folks. Be careful not to get sucked in, trying to fix or solve. Allow and acknowledge your students and move on.

Ask Reiki to come in and help you. It will. Now go ahead and start planning those classes! It's time!

What Text Should You Use in Class?

I did a lot of research before I began teaching. I holed up in Barnes and Noble for a couple of days and researched Reiki books. I also went online and studied many of the more popular Reiki teachers and textbooks. I narrowed it down to a few that really spoke to me and spent the next week or so reading them.

In the end, I chose William Rand's books from the International Center for Reiki Training (ICRT). I like his books because they are good, basic Reiki handbooks. You can find them at www.reiki.org.

I know some teachers who create their own books or binders. I thought of doing this but there was so much I didn't know in the beginning that I felt it was better to go with an established teacher.

In addition to the text, I also prepare handouts for my students. Much of what is in the handout can be found in the book, but I like the idea of layered learning. Students will hear me talk about something in class, read it in their text, and find it in their handouts. Students are bombarded with so much information in a Reiki class, it's good to give it to them in various ways to help them remember.

I arrange my handouts in a two-pocket folder. On the right side, I put together a packet with information pertinent to the class I'm teaching. A cover sheet has the agenda for the day. Behind that, I like to put useful articles that relate to that class. On the left side, I put my business card, my brochure, and my pen (with marketing information). I also include: a Reiki Code of Ethics, a lineage chart, a class review form, and a quiz (if applicable). Most of this can be found on www.reiki.org, but you will need to create your own lineage chart. A self-addressed, stamped envelope is added so they can return the quiz and review form.

I've gotten a lot of positive feedback from my students regarding the handouts. Students like a take-away. It also shows the time, effort, and love I put into planning a class. They see this and appreciate it.

One more thing: in my Reiki lineage, it is customary to give the student a small gift of gratitude for taking my class. I like to hand out crystals. I usually have a bowl that I pass around and have students chose. I've also given out candles, and copies of *Reiki News Magazine*. They love to get the gift! (As do I when I am a student.) And I am truly grateful to have been chosen as their teacher.

How Should You Structure Your Class?

This is up to you, as everyone does it differently. Think about your energy level and that of your clients. Are they older? Will one full day of Reiki be too much? Should you split it into a couple of days? I've seen Reiki Level One spaced out over three evenings, three hours each time. This is a good solution to those who work or those who aren't able to sit through a longer class. (Think older students, child care, medical issues). I've taught it over two Saturdays, with four hours each time. This was when I taught it at a local college. The room was not the most comfortable, so four-hour stints worked well.

Most of the classes I teach (and those I've attended) are full days. When I first began teaching, my classes were long. One even went ten hours! That was crazy! All were at least eight, some nine. After about five years, the classes got shorter. As I became more confident as a teacher, I didn't spend as much time talking.

In the beginning, I wanted to make sure the students *got* it. I didn't yet understand that they would not get it in one class, especially if I talked them to death. Once I actually had a woman fall asleep and snore!

It is our responsibility to attune our students and have them practice. Everything else is filler. Yes, we need to give them information and resources, but the attunement and practice are key components of the class. Remember, the best way to learn Reiki is by *doing* it, so the real work begins when they leave the classroom and begin practicing on themselves and others.

Please have your students practice. When I received my Level One and Two attunements the first time around, there was very little practice time. I left those classes very confused as to what I was supposed to do. Practice time introduces students to Reiki in a way that talking about it never can. They will leave your class more confident and with a better understanding of Reiki, if they have some practice time under their belt.

The pace of my classes follows a predictable pattern. The morning is lecture, the attunement is right before lunch, and we practice after lunch. As I mentioned, I begin and end each class with a meditation. I like the pace of this, but more often than not, I may change it, depending on the energy of the group or the guidance I receive.

Being a Virgo, I like order and a predictable sequence. When I first started teaching, I had my agenda and it was timed. If I had talkative students, I would worry if we got off schedule. I had a tendency to want to hurry the students through, so we could get back on track. What I didn't realize is that we were never off track; we were at the pace the class needed to be at.

I since have learned to be in that flow, but it took years. It took trust and me growing into myself as a teacher to be able to do this. I no longer worry if I have talky students. That's not to say I still don't have to direct the flow on occasion, but it's different. It is much, much easier and a lot more fun. There are some classes that are so turned around and out of order that it would have given me a heart attack in the earlier days. Now I just go with the flow. Everyone is happier. Trust Reiki. Trust yourself.

Remember that Reiki will work through you and that it's not coming from you. It's not about you; it's about the Reiki. This is perhaps the biggest lesson I had to learn and it took me a long time. My ego got in the way and that fear was ever present. Even though I was Doing It Afraid, I see now, in retrospect, that I was still a prisoner of fear, that I wasn't allowing myself the freedom to really be in the flow, to let go of the control.

And remember that you are the teacher and the student. Every student has something to teach us if we are open to the message.

How Much Time Between Levels?

When I started taking classes, I was told that I should wait at least six months between Level One and Two and at least a year between Level Two and Master. That was in 2002. (This differs between lineages and teachers.) I followed these guidelines and I'm glad I did. I wasn't in a hurry and waiting allowed the energies of the attunements to settle in. After I got Master Practitioner, I waited a year and took it again along with Master Teacher. Then I waited a year before taking my Karuna Master class.

This is something I struggled with when I started teaching. One of my first students wanted to zip through the levels. I knew her and it was my opinion that she was going too fast, that her ego was engaged and she wanted to be a Reiki Master as soon as possible. I told her I felt she should wait. She got upset and ended up studying with another teacher.

As the years went by, I noticed more and more students wanting to take Level Two right after Level One. Many teachers taught Level One and Two back to back on the same weekend. I spoke with my teachers and colleagues about this and the consensus was that it really was not up to us (teachers) when the student took a class.

I eventually came around to this type of thinking and no longer tell students they aren't ready. If someone wants to take a class, I include that person. I have to assume the person knows what he or she is doing. Reiki will work with people to give them what they need. And while I am okay with this, I do state in classes that I feel it is important to put some time in between the levels, that one should respect the energy of Reiki and give it time to settle in.

Don't rush through the levels. Take your time and get to know Reiki. It's not going anywhere, so why hurry? But after all is said and done, I leave the decision with the student. It has been my experience that if someone is not ready something will prevent him or her from coming to a class. Reiki knows what it is doing. Remember Reiki is the teacher!

Some Thoughts and Experiences on Teaching

Now I'd like to share some additional thoughts and experiences on teaching. You may recognize yourself in these examples and they may help you to feel validated. I hope you can learn from my mistakes and examples and if you remember anything, please remember to go easy on yourself when you start teaching. Have compassion for yourself and know you are doing the best that you can. You have to begin somewhere.

Anne Lamott is one of my favorite writers and I love how she says to just show up, put your butt in the chair, and write your shitty first draft. So go out and teach your shitty first class. Of course it won't be, but you may feel that way. Learn how to show up, to Do It Afraid, and to exercise that teaching muscle. You can do it. What's the alternative? You don't want to stay in that land of longing and regret. Get out there! You just might surprise yourself.

We are Always Students, Even When Teaching

Put your ego aside and pay attention to your students. I can't stress enough how much they have to teach us. You might think you are teaching a Reiki class, and it appears that you are, but so much more is going on. Your responsibility as a teacher is to attune the students to the desired level and to give them tools and resources. What they do with that is up to them. And please don't worry about what they do with the information after they leave. Yes, you can be there for them if they ask you to be (key) but don't follow them around or assume that they are going to be just like you and get mad when they are not. (I did that.)

In every single class I have taught there has been a healing opportunity for me. As long as we are open to letting our students be those highly polished mirrors reflecting back to us what we need to learn, the opportunity is there. If you are already teaching, think about those students who drive you crazy, who you consider high maintenance or you don't care for as much as the others. Yes, even Reiki Masters do this. We are human and Reiki can help us to heal this.

Why do they drive you crazy? What is it about them? Are you sure you don't see a little bit of yourself there? It's worth considering. You might not like what you discover but if you really allow yourself to be open to this idea, you can learn so much about yourself.

To Take Advice or Not

Sometimes students will offer suggestions that are inappropriate or not a good fit for a class. I am learning how to navigate these requests. Two recent examples that come to mind are one student continuously telling me that I needed to raise my prices, that I don't charge enough and that she felt I did not value my services. Another student suggested it would be more professional if I gave each student a full Reiki treatment during the class instead of having them practice on each other. I'm learning some valuable lessons as a result of these suggestions.

- I have more confidence in my teaching than I realized, and I do not need to respond in a defensive way. I can come from a place of grace, thank the student, and later consider the request and decide whether or not it has merit.

- I can look at why this request has a charge for me. Am I feeling threatened or defensive? If so, why?

- I can realize that sometimes in a Reiki class, students' own issues arise, and what they are saying has way more to do with them than me. I can be a compassionate listener and keep the class moving forward, instead of becoming emotionally involved and taking it personally. Don't let yourself get sucked in!

And to come clean and be perfectly honest, when I first heard the two comments I've given as examples, my confidence was shaken and I became upset. I reacted and worried about myself as a professional, I made it about me. After a bit, this feeling lessened and I thought about the points I'm sharing with you now, but I did not go there right away. It is my intention to get to this place of grace sooner, instead of letting my ego get in the way.

Suggestions for New Teachers

Reiki teachers are human and even the best of us have days and classes that can be challenging. A Reiki classroom can be a charged environment, for both the teacher and the student. This for me was the most challenging part of teaching a class.

In the beginning, I was exhausted after teaching a class. I would have to go to bed. My mind was fried, my body was tired and I couldn't see straight. This happened the first three months or so until I realized that I was using all of my energy trying to control things. I was striving for perfection, as I did in most areas of my life at the time. I didn't realize it was due to my fear and need to control.

Nor was I allowing myself to be in the flow. I was feeling reactive to my students and because I didn't want them to know this I kept it in. Doing that all day was exhausting! Looking back on it from the vantage point of teaching for many years it seems unreal, but that is how it was. I wanted to appear perfect and unruffled, like my teacher, or I should say how I perceived her to be. I was striving for something that did not exist, but like I always say, we don't know what we don't know.

I'm not sure how or when it came to me but I eventually relaxed. Like Anne Lamott's advice about those "shitty first drafts," I think I had to teach a bunch of shitty first classes to get it right. And it wasn't the content or quality of the class that suffered. It was me, or more accurately, my ego and personality. They were on display big time. It was the Deb Show after all. I made it all about me. MY class. MY way. MY! MY! MY! Oh, my!

I got sick of myself and my big show pretty quick. I discovered that just like in the Reiki room when I worked on a client, it was much better when I was myself and not some image I was trying to emulate. When I admitted I didn't know something or apologized and owned my reactive behavior the students seemed to like it. They relaxed when I relaxed and it made for a much smoother flow in the class. It got better as I became more comfortable with the process.

Now I pretty much have no plan when I teach a class. I send Reiki ahead of time, meet the students where they are and stay open to the guidance. Quite a change for this control freak Virgo! And guess what? It works! Try it! It took me some time and many, many classes to learn this, but once I became aware of my behavior it was easier to do.

Give yourself an honest look-see. Allow yourself to discover your triggers and reactive behavior. Ask Reiki to help you. You will be on your way to healing and being a much better teacher. You are also modeling good behavior to your students. The teachers I respect the most are the ones that allow their human side to surface. They are real. I challenge you to be too, for your own sake.

My First Class

I was well trained, and had a few years of practice under my belt before I began teaching, yet I didn't feel prepared for that first class. Organizationally I was fine. My prior training as a meeting planner and office manager served me well when getting ready for classes. Mentally and emotionally, though, I was a mess. I remember how nervous I was when the doorbell rang and the first student walked in.

In retrospect, I can see I had little or no self-confidence and trust. I let myself believe it was *me* guiding the class, and not the Reiki. I had not yet learned to send distant Reiki to the class beforehand. I tried to control everything: the time, the conversation, and the pace of the class. I spent a lot of energy spinning my wheels, when the students could have been better served by my going with the flow.

The class was not horrible. I had a great outline, good books and resources, and felt comfortable with the attunement process. In fact, that was my favorite part I love how that felt, passing on the Reiki energy, opening it up for others to walk this path. My heart was bursting with love and gratitude, and I felt so lucky to be in a position to do this. So what was wrong? Why was I so angst-ridden? This certainly was not good modeling behavior. In a nutshell, ego and personality were to blame.

One of the things my teachers continuously stressed in training was to keep our egos and personalities out of our practice. I did not quite understand what this meant, but in time I have come to understand it.

While it was my intention to offer Reiki instruction and pass attunements, on some other level I wanted the students to like me. I wanted them to like the way I taught. I wanted to be the best and brightest Reiki Teacher ever! And while I do truly want to shine with the light of Reiki, this was different. I wasn't coming from my best and highest place. I was coming from that place of fear and ego, and if I am honest, it came through in my teaching.

I beat myself up badly after that first class. Instead of focusing on what the students learned and that five women were newly attuned and spreading their Reiki light, I worried about what I said or did not say. I worried that they didn't like me, that they would tell others I was a bad teacher. I worried that I would get a bad reputation in the Reiki community. I'm embarrassed to admit this, but it is how I felt at the time. I remember sending an email to my teacher, gushing about all of this. She wrote me back a long and loving email and reminded me about ego and personality.

The light bulb finally went on, and I began to understand how I needed to take a step back, to take myself out of the equation, and begin trusting the Reiki energy. It seems so obvious now, but at the time I didn't have a clue. I am so grateful for her loving guidance.

Reiki Takes Control (instead of me)

I began to send distant Reiki to my classes beforehand, starting about a week before each class, and repeated it daily. I'd ask that my ego and personality step aside and allow the Reiki energy to give each and every one of us what we need, and to trust that. I also reframed the way I felt about teaching. I decided to not think of it as teaching, but rather as sharing something that I loved and did every day. After all, I did do Reiki every day and I did love it. I was living proof of how it has the ability to change our lives.

Some Thoughts & Experiences on Teaching

This took tremendous pressure off me. I no longer had to "control" the classes. The day of each class, I felt the Reiki energy there, waiting for us. It was welcoming and comforting. And while I used the book and the outline, I was more comfortable sharing my experiences. I also remembered something I had heard and now live by: I am not the teacher. Reiki is the teacher. I am a channel. I am giving my students information and providing them opportunities to study and practice Reiki, but Reiki is the teacher. Talk about *relief!*

I had never taught anything before teaching Reiki. I was more of a behind-the-scenes type of person, not comfortable in the limelight. Reiki helped me to overcome this fear and heal my insecurity. Bit by bit my confidence grew and I became more excited and creative.

If you teach, listen to the Reiki. If you are fearful, surrender to the Reiki and allow it to guide you and teach you. Pay attention to your heart and gut, and let your head, ego, and personality take a break. It's not really you.

Asserting Yourself as a Teacher

I was teaching for about a year when I had quite an experience in a Reiki Level One class. It was a class of five, all women I knew. I had them lined up and as I was doing the final part of the attunement the last person started to freak out. She began to bat away my hands and say she was done, so I finished up quickly.

We took a lunch break and I was hoping that things would settle down but they did not. A few of the other students were picking up her anxiety. I left the room to compose myself and all of a sudden I had a vision of her throwing up and I knew she had to leave the class. I came back into the room and told this student she had to go home. She asked if she could stay for the rest of the class, but just lie on the couch. I said no, she had to go now. It was really hard for me to do this. I was afraid to ask her to leave but knew it was necessary, for her and for the class. She called her brother, who came to pick her up. The minute she got into his car she began to throw up and didn't stop for some time. It turns out she had the flu. After a day or so she was fine.

Still, the fear of the attunement process stayed in her mind and she connected it to her illness. She signed up for the Level Two class a few months later, but wasn't sure she could go through with it. I saw her for a Reiki session a few days before the class and at the end of her session I got the guidance to give her the Level Two attunement right there. She wasn't waiting for it and she was calm and relaxed after her session. After the attunement, which went very well, she laughed and said she had been thinking of asking me to do this but was afraid. I'm glad I trusted my guidance and went ahead with it. She took the class and had no trouble with that attunement, and went on to take Master and Master Teacher with no problem.

As a new teacher I was afraid to rock the boat or upset a student, but I knew I had to take guided action. This was a new way for me to be and a good lesson. When you are faced with difficult decisions in a class or with a client, always ask Reiki for help and listen to and trust your guidance. And always come from your heart.

Help Your Students to Help Themselves

When I was a new teacher, I wanted to be able to answer every single question. I wanted to be the best teacher, the one who knew everything! I was going to be accessible, available, *there* for them! I was going to take their hand and gently lead them on their path. I didn't want them to have to recreate the wheel; after all, if I knew the answers, why not help them? I honestly believed that this is what a good teacher did. And while it is a good idea to make ourselves available as teachers, it's even better to teach students to rely on themselves and their discoveries. It was my fear of being thought of as a bad teacher that had motivated me to do other than this. I now am better able to discern the difference.

As a newer teacher, if I didn't know the answer to a question, I was afraid my students would think less of me. My insecurity as a teacher really came screaming out. I didn't realize it was okay to simply say, "I don't know." I once asked a Reiki colleague what she did when she didn't know the answer to a question. Her answer: "I make something up." Really? It took a few years but I have gotten to the point where I am very comfortable saying, "I don't know."

I remember reading in the ICRT ART/Master manual that a worthy goal for all Reiki Masters is to become the kind of Reiki Master you would like to have as your Reiki Master. And I realized I'd respect the type of teacher that said, "I don't know" because that is honest. I've also grown to understand, respect, and admire the teacher that turns the question back to the student and asks her to sit with her question, to ask Reiki.

The other day I taught a one-on-one Master/Teacher class. These one-on-one classes can be somewhat challenging. The student had requested it, and it had been a long while since I'd done one; I was looking forward to it. It was a long day filled with many questions. Some I was able to answer, some I said I didn't know, and some I felt comfortable lobbing back to the student. At the end of the day, I felt happy and satisfied and saw my growth as a teacher. In none of those instances did I second-guess or question myself. I trusted.

Work With a Variety of Teachers

I studied with a lot of different teachers. It was a valuable learning experience and it helped me tremendously as a teacher. There are so many styles and lineages, and everyone teaches differently. I believe we gravitate towards those that match our vibration. I popped around my first spin through the levels and that offered me some unique and different experiences. The classes were small and I was able to really pay attention. From these teachers, I learned how I would teach and also the things I would do differently. This is not a judgment on those teachers, as I believe I got what I needed. Each of my teachers helped me to be the teacher I am today.

Find your own style and be true to yourself. Try not to compare yourself with others or compete. This is hard, or at least for me it was hard in the beginning. My ego was actively engaged. I felt myself "better" than some teachers because I was so thorough, even though I really didn't have a clue. I also felt I would never measure up to some of my teachers and let that intimidate me. Now I just do the best I can, meet the students where they are, and let Reiki guide the class. When you do that, everything flows.

Class Outlines

What follows are class outlines and information about each level of Reiki as I've taught it over the years. I don't always teach each class the same way. While I do go over everything in the outline, the energy of the class usually dictates the order in which I do things. Trust your instincts and the energy of the class and go with the flow. When I first started teaching I was so nervous and I stuck to this outline no matter what. I think it helped me to feel safe and in control. Of course, that is an illusion but after a bit I began really paying attention to the student's needs and I learned to meet them where they were and things flowed much better. Don't be afraid to experiment.

The following outlines are pre-Holy Fire. The way I teach now has changed since receiving that energy. To learn more about Holy Fire, please go to www.reiki.org.

Reiki Level One Class Agenda

Text: *Reiki, The Healing Touch: First and Second Degree Manual* by
      William Lee Rand
(Duration: 9 a.m. to 6 p.m.)
Sign in
Opening meditation
Introductions
Overview of day
Definition of Reiki
History of Reiki
Pre-attunement hands-on experience
Chakra overview/meditation
Receive attunement
Lunch (Share/Q&A)
Learn and practice self-treatment hand positions
Learn hand positions to give a Reiki treatment to others
Practice
Wrap up/discussion
Closing meditation
Evaluations
Certificates

When I send out confirmation emails to the students, I include the above agenda to give them an idea of what to expect. I try to email the confirmations and agenda a month before the class. At that time, I require a non-refundable (but reusable) deposit to hold their space in the class. I also invite them to contact me if they have any questions.

Class Outlines

Students are asked to arrive 15 minutes prior to the beginning of each class so we can begin promptly at the stated time. This allows for bad traffic, unexpected delays or those that are perennially late. After they arrive I have them sign in (name, address, phone, email) and pay their balance for the class. I accept check or cash payments for class. I invite them to make a cup of tea and ask them to find a space and make themselves comfortable.

I begin the class with a meditation. Over the years I've used different meditations to open the class. They are usually brief, less then five minutes and I read the meditation to the students. This helps them to relax and settle into the class. Introductions follow, and then a brief overview of the day.

The text I use for Level One and Two is *Reiki The Healing Touch, First and Second Degree Manual* by William Lee Rand. I talk briefly about why I chose this book.

One of the things I did that really helps me in my teaching, especially as a new teacher, was to create a binder for each class. In that binder is my class outline and then notes about what I plan to talk about. It helps me to remember everything, especially if I get swept up in the class and get off track. It also serves as a safety blanket, as I like the feel of it in my hands.

I will then give a brief history of Reiki; what it is and is not, do an energy exercise, followed by a talk on the chakras. After I am done speaking I like to put on Doreen Virtue's CD *Chakra Clearing*. This is a short, 20 minute guided meditation. It takes the student on a journey of their chakras, explaining and clearing each one.

When the meditation ends, I segue right into the attunement. The students are calm and relaxed. I ask them to sit in *gassho* (a Japanese Reiki Technique) and I explain the attunement process to them. I then state my intention and perform the Level One attunement. After the attunement, I ask them to hold the silence for 15 minutes. They can sit quietly, go outside for a walk, or write about their experience.

Lunch comes next. Most of the time we stay in and eat. The students have brought their lunch and this is a nice time to connect, share experiences or ask questions. Sometimes we do a potluck.

After lunch I teach the students how to conduct a full self-healing session. I walk them through it, spending about 5 minutes on each hand position. There are pictures in their book but I tell them that when they do this on their own to practice as they are guided. I want them to get a feel for the energy. The pictures are there as a template to get them started. This self-healing session takes about an hour. I talk a lot about the importance of doing daily self-healing and encourage them to keep it up after class. Their "homework" is to practice self-healing for the next 21 days.

Many times I hear "But I don't have time!" I tell them to make the time. Really? You don't have time? Not even ½ hour to give yourself Reiki? I bet there is something in our day that we can take away to make room for the Reiki. If they swear that they really don't have time I ask them to put their hands on themselves when they lie down at night and/or when they wake up in the morning. Just lie there a few extra minutes and give yourself Reiki. It is the least you can do for yourself. Most students love the idea of self-Reiki and this kicks off their daily practice.

After the self-healing session we go to the table to practice. Each student takes a turn lying on the table with the others practicing. Depending on the class and the time, we do 10, 15 or 20-minute rounds. If it's a one on one class the student will practice with me and we do 30 minutes each.

When I first began teaching I told the students which hand positions to use and I timed them. This has evolved over the years where I now encourage them to feel their own way around the table. I only time the session, not the time between hand positions. I believe this empowers the student to discern the subtle energies and begin to trust themselves in the process.

Sometimes I will have a class that does not want to practice on the table. When I was teaching the patients and staff at the cancer center where I worked they did not want to do the table work. They were there to learn how to do Reiki on themselves, or in the case of a caregiver, their loved one, but were not comfortable working on each other on the table. What I did was set up chairs and had them team up 2x2 and practice on each other's heads and shoulders. It wasn't as intimate or intimidating yet they were still able to get some practice in and begin to feel Reiki's energy flow.

When I taught in the colleges or Park and Rec the classes were larger and I didn't have my table there, so I also employed the chair method. The students paired up and worked on each other's heads, necks, shoulders, hearts and arms. It was enough practice for them to get the feel of it. You can give someone an entire Reiki session while they are seated in a chair. Be creative!

After the practice we get together for one final Q&A discussion. I end the class with another short, guided meditation that I read. I then pass out their certificates and a class review form. Class is over! Congratulations! You did it!

Reiki Level Two Class Agenda

Text: *Reiki, The Healing Touch: First and Second Degree Manual*
    by William Lee Rand
(Duration: 9 a.m. to 6 p.m.)
Sign in
Opening meditation
Introductions
Overview of day
Reiki symbols
Receive attunement
Lunch   (Share/Q&A)
Japanese Reiki Techniques
Distance healing exercises
Hands-on practice using the symbols with a partner
Symbols quiz (take-home)
Wrap up/discussion
Closing Meditation
Evaluations
Certificates

Level Two is a very fun and exciting class to teach. The student already has a familiarity with Reiki and it becomes a bit more tangible, as we learn how to use the symbols to assist us in our daily lives.

My Reiki Level Two class runs much the same way as my Reiki Level One class. I ask the students to arrive 15 minutes prior to the start time. I have them sign in, pay, invite them to get something to drink and make themselves comfortable. Again, I begin the class with a brief meditation that I read to them.

Class Outlines

After the meditation I ask the students to introduce themselves to each other. I ask them to state their name, tell me what brought them to the Level Two class and then to tell me something they like about themselves today. I learned to ask that question from my teacher, who uses it with her students. It can be very revealing!

I go over what we'll be doing in class that day and ask if anyone has any questions with regards to Level One. I also ask if they have been doing self-healing and I encourage them to share their experiences.

Next I introduce them to the Level Two symbols. The best advice I ever got from my Reiki teacher about the symbols was, "develop a relationship with the symbols." When she said this in class I totally got it. I like to think of the symbols as little people, each with their own distinct personality. They are here to help us. Use them! I know so many Reiki Masters that don't use the symbols. I know so many students that forget to use the symbols. I can't stress enough how important they are in your practice. Why wouldn't you use these powerful tools that are literally at your fingertips?

I have the students spend some time drawing the symbols. I provide the paper and give them about half an hour. I also go over the names of the symbols, having the students recite the names of them out loud, over and over until they feel comfortable with them. Sometimes students are shy and this can take a while, but I keep it going, giving them a chance to lose the fear and to welcome the symbols into their lives.

Once they feel comfortable, we stand and I teach them how to "strengthen their light" using the power symbol, CKR. The idea behind strengthening their light is that instead of surrounding themselves with the white light of love and protection, they tap into their own light and strengthen it using the power symbol. This means that anything less than light will not be attracted to them. Teflon Reiki!

To strengthen your light you draw a large CKR out in front of you, and then beam it into yourself, saying three times, CKR, CKR, CKR. You do the same at each chakra, starting at the root, and going all the way up to the crown, each time drawing a smaller CKR at each chakra, beaming it in and saying CKR, CKR, CKR. I then ask them to put CKR on their palms and pat three times, saying the name each time they pat.

Together we then send CKR to the four directions, the heavens and the earth. Even though they are not yet attuned I want them to be aware of this symbol and some of its uses. Once this is done I ask them to take a seat and I give them the Reiki Level Two attunement.

After the attunement, I ask them to hold the silence for 15 minutes and either journal, walk outside, or sit quietly. Lunch follows and again it is a good time to connect, ask questions, and share experiences.

In the afternoon, I talk about the Japanese Reiki Techniques and show them where to find the information in the book. Next, I teach the students how to send Reiki to the past, present and future using the distant symbol (HSZSN).

For this exercise, I pass out index cards and ask students to write the name of a person they know who would accept this distant Reiki healing. I then ask them to draw the three symbols they just received on the back of the card (more practice).

I have them sit in *gassho* (a Japanese Reiki Technique) with the card between their prayer hands and we meditate and send Reiki. I tell them I see it as a bridge of light between myself and the person I am sending it to, from my heart to the other's, while I quietly chant HSZSN to myself. I share this example as one way to do it, but students can choose any way they are guided. We sit in meditation for at least five minutes, sometimes more. I encourage them to do this for longer periods of time when they practice at home.

Next we send Reiki to our past. We can't change our past but we can change the energy around it, how we remember it and energetically release those old wounds. I ask them to think of something they would like healed, physically, mentally, emotionally or spiritually and write it down on the index card, and then draw the three Level Two symbols on the back. Again we sit in *gassho* and send Reiki to our past. We do this for five minutes but I encourage them to do this for longer periods of time when they practice at home.

* * * * *

I vaguely remember being taught to send the distant symbol (HSZSN) to my past the first time I had my Level Two training and while the teacher might have talked about doing some of these exercises, we did not practice how to use the symbols. When I took my second Master class my teacher talked about using HSZSN, the distant symbol to send Reiki to your past. It really had a profound, life changing impact on me. I'd like to share that experience with you now.

During the lunch break of my Master class our teacher was talking about the inner child. I remember rolling my eyes and thinking "oh jeez, here we go again with this new age stuff!" I didn't believe in or understand this inner child business and really did think it was hooey! I shared with the teacher that I had recently been asked to give Reiki to a 10-year-old girl and I told her mother I could not.

At the time, I felt very strongly that I didn't want to. I had no desire to work with children. It never occurred to me that there could be a trigger there until my teacher suggested I might want to explore my inner child issues. Immediately I became defensive and said I didn't have any. I'm childlike! I play with kids! I can tap into the kid in me! Sheesh!

After lunch the class did a meditation and I met my inner child. She was a wounded ten-year-old girl, sad and hurt, full of shame and anxiety. I began to cry and pretty much cried the rest of the day.

When I got home, I decided to do a healing with the distant symbol, HSZSN. Every Sunday, from June-August I went out into the woods behind my home and sent HSZSN to my ten year old self. I'd walk in the woods and chant and Reiki transported me back to that place, in 1964, where my fear and shame and anxiety were born. This was a rough time for me, and I never realized how much of those feelings I internalized and were still with me. That poor child!

Every Sunday, I would walk and chant and cry and every Sunday I would feel that little girl's pain. I slogged through that summer, allowing myself to feel those feelings, knowing I was healing. By the end of the summer the tears were gone and I was able to integrate my ten-year-old self into my adult self. It was a wonderful healing and it helped me to better understand myself. HSZSN is such a powerful healing tool. You might want to try this. Think of those times from your past that you would like healed and give it a whirl.

* * * * *

Lastly we send Reiki to our future. The students are instructed to write down an upcoming event or goal on the front of the index card and draw the three symbols on the back, sit in *gassho* and send Reiki to their future. I love this practice as it has taught me how to trust. When I send Reiki to my future I no longer have to worry about it. When I show up I know Reiki will be there, keeping me safe, guided, protected and loved.

After these exercises, we take a break and then head to the table for a few hours of hands on practice. I encourage them to play around with their new symbols, asking them to pay attention to the subtle frequencies of each symbol. It's the beginning of a now relationship.

After the practice, we do one final Q&A discussion and one last, brief guided meditation that I read to the students. I pass out the certificates and class review form. We are done! Before they leave I encourage them to continue with their daily self-healing practice and to begin using the symbols in the form of drawing, chanting, writing, however they learn best. Homework!

Reiki Master Practitioner Class Agenda

Text: *Advanced Reiki Training Manual* by William Lee Rand
(Duration: 9 a.m. to 6 p.m.)
Sign in
Opening meditation
Introductions
Overview of class
Contemplating the implications of being a Reiki Master, living Reiki, being Reiki:

- What does becoming a Reiki Master mean to you?

- Why are you moving on to this level?

- Where do you see yourself going with this?

Review of Levels One and Two and symbols
Introduction of the Master Symbol, use and practice
Longer meditation
Attunement
Lunch (Share/Q&A)
Your Reiki practice
Crystal grid
Aura clearing
Symbols quiz (take-home)
Closing meditation
Evaluations
Certificates

Class Outlines

The Master Level can be done a number of ways as it differs between lineages. The first time I took Master Practitioner it was a one-day stand-alone class. I received the master symbol. I didn't plan on teaching so I didn't do Master/Teacher at that time. The training was about six hours. It was a one on one class and this seemed to be enough time. There was a lot of meditation and an attunement to the master symbol. I stayed at this level for a year and this is when I began my practice at the spa. About a year later I desired the Master/Teacher attunement even though I wasn't planning to teach. Something was calling me and I am glad I listened.

I took Master/Teacher with my current teachers. They teach it over three full days. The first day of the training is ART (Advanced Reiki Techniques, same as Master Practitioner) and the next two days is Master/Teacher.

When I teach Master Practitioner, it is as a stand-alone class, as I learned it. Depending on the number of students the time can range from six to eight hours. I take up to six students and the more students there are, the longer the class may go, due to sharing, although this is not always the case. Most of my classes are small and intimate and in this class in particular, there is a lot of sharing.

After the students have settled in, I begin the class with a short meditation. I ask the students to introduce themselves and say why they were guided to this class and something they like about themselves.

I go over the outline for the day and then the students share what it means to them to be a Reiki Master. This can generate a lot of really interesting discussion and I allow plenty of time for it.

There is a brief review of the previous levels and symbols that came before this level and this is a good time for the students to ask any questions or share experiences they have had up to now. Again, it's an interesting discussion and I like that the students are doing most of the talking, discovering and remembering what they know about Reiki. It has been my experience and that of watching others that most of us know more than we think we do about Reiki. This can be a very interesting and empowering discussion.

Next on the agenda is a longer meditation. One I like to use is *Infinite Spectrum* by my teacher, Laurelle Gaia.

The students are really in the flow after this meditation, so we go right into the attunement. Afterwards I ask them to hold the silence for 15 minutes to allow everyone to integrate the energies they just received.

Now it's time for lunch and another opportunity to bond, share experiences and ask questions.

The afternoon is a mix of discussion and practice. We begin by talking about Reiki practices. At this point in their process, the students may be thinking about practicing Reiki in the community or starting their own practice. It's a good time to flesh out their feelings and to answer any questions they may have. Even if they are not consciously aware of it, this is a good time to plant seeds, as one never knows where Reiki might lead. It can't hurt to put it out there.

Now for some practice and fun! The Reiki grid makes its debut. Over the years how I teach this has evolved. I now gift the students with small crystals so they can make their own grids. This makes it more real and it's something they can take away and continue to practice. You might want to consider doing this. It also lessens the self-consciousness that comes with practice, as they are all practicing together on their own grids, as opposed to them watching each other practice on my grid. This also ensures they will have a grid to work with when they get home. Creating good Reiki habits here!

Next I talk about and demonstrate aura clearing. Then the students pair up and practice as I guide them through the process.

We do a final Q&A discussion. I recap what we've learned and ask for any last questions, comments or observations.

Our ending meditation is the Reiki Master Moving Meditation. It's a physical meditation, using our bodies, much like a Tai Chi exercise. I demonstrate it first and then we all practice it together. This is a very empowering exercise and I encourage them to do this daily. I believe it really puts us in that Master place.

Certificates and class review forms follow and we are done. Another level completed with more Reiki Masters out in the world!

Reiki Master/Teacher Class Agenda

Text: *Reiki Master Manual* by William Lee Rand
(Duration: 9 a.m. to 6 p.m.)
Sign in
Opening meditation
Introductions
Class overview
Review of previous levels and symbols
Introduction to the Tibetan symbols, use and practice
Longer meditation
Attunement
Lunch
How to Pass attunements
> Hui Yin
> Violet Breath
> Healing Attunement

Passing attunements practice
Symbols quiz (take-home)
Q&A
Closing meditation
Evaluations
Certificate

I teach Master/Teacher in one long day. We start the day with a light meditation to center everyone and get us ready for the day. I go over the agenda and we do introductions. I ask the students what brought them to this level, where they received their previous levels and to tell the class something they like about themselves.

We are now ready to rock and roll! We do a review of the symbols we have learned up to this point. Sometimes students who studied with other teachers will have different symbols. I encourage them to use the symbols they were attuned to, that it does not matter if they look different, the intention is what makes the symbols work, once they are attuned to them.

After the review I introduce them to the Tibetan symbols and we spend some time chanting and drawing them, along with the other symbols. It is important that they are comfortable with the symbols and really know them, as they will be passing attunements later in the day.

A longer meditation follows, which flows nicely into the attunement. Afterwards we have a silent period of reflection to integrate those energies they just received.

Lunch follows. This is a good opportunity to share experiences, ask questions and relax.

After lunch I walk the students through the steps of how to pass an attunement. I break it down into manageable segments and show them before I have them practice. This part of the class can cause performance anxiety so I pair them up and have them work together. This way they are not "on stage". We spend the afternoon passing attunements for all of the levels, including the healing attunement.

If there is only one student in the class I have a large stuffed monkey for them to partner with. He has long arms and legs, and they are able to practice with him as they would on another person. I need to be free to coach the student through the process.

An excellent tool to assist you in teaching passing attunements is *The Reiki Practicum* by Laurelle Gaia. This is such a helpful tool, both to me and to my students, as they are walked through all levels of the attunement process. I play the CD and it can be stopped or started to keep pace with the students. As the teacher I can focus on the students and not worry about reading the instructions. The CD has all levels of attunements, including the healing attunement. I highly recommend it.

When we are finished we take a well-deserved break and a question and answer/discussion period follows. A brief closing meditation ends the class and afterwards I pass out the class review form and their certificates.

These examples should help you to get started on your classes. Good luck, have fun and don't forget to meet your students where they are. Trust that the Reiki energy will direct the class, not you! That should take some pressure off.

Additional Reiki Classes

In many lineages the Reiki Master/Teacher class is the highest level of Reiki one can attain. I took my training with the International Center for Reiki Training (ICRT) and they have additional levels of Reiki. I mention them below but do not go into detail. If you would like more information about Karuna Reiki® or Holy Fire Reiki please go to www.Reiki.org, the website for the ICRT.

Karuna Reiki®

A year after my Master/Teacher training I took a Karuna Reiki® class with the same teachers. I wanted to learn more and was excited about adding more symbols to my practice. Karuna Reiki® comes from William Rand, the founder of the International Center for Reiki Training. *Karuna* is a Sanskrit word that can be translated as "compassionate action," bringing more compassion to yourself and others. This level of Reiki training can open you up to work more closely with enlightened beings. I met Quan Yin as a result of my Karuna training and she has been one of my guides ever since.

I experienced deep healing as a result of this level and began to understand and meet many new guides. Chanting and toning are a part of Karuna Reiki®. It's quite liberating to work with the symbols in this way. I'd also like to recommend *The Book on Karuna Reiki®* by Laurelle Shanti Gaia. You may want to consider moving on to Karuna Reiki® to expand your practice and bring this new level of energy into your life.

Holy Fire Reiki

Another form of Reiki that has recently been introduced by the International Center for Reiki Training is Holy Fire Reiki. A definition that I like to use is "Holy Fire Reiki is a spiritual energy that provides purification, healing, empowerment and guidance." I see and feel it as a higher level of consciousness and like Karuna Reiki® it introduces us to new guides and higher vibrational awareness.

I believe Holy Fire Reiki to be a natural extension of the levels. Before I'd heard about it I was yearning for something more. This feeling has been expressed by many of my students as well. It is a very loving, safe energy and it continues to develop itself to be more evolved and effective. Holy Fire Reiki is taught in both the Usui and Karuna levels.

Even though I was yearning for something more, I was initially reluctant to move on to this level, fearing change. I was comfortable in my practice and wasn't sure I was ready for it. Yet my intuition very strongly guided me to take it. I'm grateful I listened to that guidance. The Holy Fire classes are so different and from a teacher's perspective I worried so much before I taught the first one. I needn't have. It has been my experience that the Holy Fire classes teach themselves. There is such divine guidance at work in these classes.

Holy Fire has changed the way I practice Reiki, teach Reiki and the way I live. It is that powerful. I highly recommend it. I have been actively working with its energy since I received it. It's an amazing energy, nothing like I've ever experienced. It's been almost two years since that first Holy Fire class, and I'm feeling so light filled, so free, so grounded and aligned. I encourage you to check it out.

QUESTIONS TO PONDER CHECKLIST

☐ Do you have the confidence to teach? If not, are you willing to Do It Afraid? Explore your feelings around teaching.

☐ Have you been asked to teach? What did you say? How did it make you feel? You may never feel ready, so just jump in and do it!

☐ If the word teaching scares you, rephrase it to take out the charge it has for you. Think of it as sharing what you love— sharing Reiki.

☐ Get a calendar and set your class dates for the next six months. Start with one day a month or more if you are guided.

☐ Chose a meditation to begin and end your class. Use a guided meditation from a CD, read something, or create your own.

☐ Explore how you would like to teach. What best suits you— formal or informal?

☐ If you choose to teach formally, do your research and create your class outlines. Spend time reading the books of other teachers as you develop your own class and choose a text.

☐ What are your strengths and weaknesses in the area of teaching? Ask Reiki to help you discover what they are and ask for opportunities for healing. What do you bring to the table?

☐ When you start teaching, remember to use your distant Reiki. Send it to the class and the students (and yourself) ahead of time. It will meet you there and guide the class.

☐ Learn how to meet your students where they are.

☐ Let go of control! Trust the process!

Wrapping Up

*P*ut your hands on the person and get out of the way. That is the best advice I've ever received about Reiki. This is the way you allow Reiki to master you. You learn how to trust and to be in the flow. You can read a million books but until you surrender and allow yourself to be in the flow of that beautiful life force energy you really can't know it.

Still, you need more than this to run a successful Reiki business. Yesterday someone asked me to share the ingredients that make up a thriving Reiki practice. I thought about it and, a few things stood out: communication, respect, being your authentic self, and knowing good business practices. And of course, using Reiki.

All of this is possible and none of it is really that difficult. It requires you to be your best self at all times. Those times you are not, it requires you to acknowledge it and make amends. Tell the truth. Treat people as you wish to be treated. Speak from your heart. Put your ego and personality aside and allow Reiki to master you. All traits are worthy of a good Reiki Master. Be that Reiki Master you wish to study with!

You can learn good business practices. When I was in recruiting back in corporate America, our team looked for people that had those values. The rest can be taught. You can learn the nuts and bolts of how to create and sustain a thriving Reiki practice, but those other things have to come from inside of you. If you can't find them, do your inner work. Ask Reiki to help you. This is crucial and ongoing; so I'll say it again, do your work. If you do, you may find your own peaceful world. Onward!

Reiki Resources

Below is a list of websites and books that I used as a new Reiki teacher and practitioner. Most of them are Reiki related but a few are some of my favorites that I discovered around the time I met Reiki and they've helped me to learn how to *be present* in my new life. I've used many more books over the years but these were the ones that got me started on my Reiki path.

One of the things I did for my clients and students was to keep a list of resources and a shelf of books I let them borrow. I would go to Half-Price books or garage sales and buy multiple copies of some of these books. It was a lending library of sorts and it helped many of my clients and students on their path. I love to share what has worked for me. I love to see others succeed.

Websites:

www.reiki.org
The International Center for Reiki Training

www.iarp.org
International Association of Reiki Professionals

www.reikiclasses.com
My Reiki teacher's website

www.reikiinmedicine.org
Website of Pamela Miles, a good medical Reiki resource

www.reikirays.com
Your Daily Source of Reiki Inspiration

Books

Reiki—A Comprehensive Guide by Pamela Miles

Essential Reiki—A Complete Guide to an Ancient Healing Art
by Diane Stein

Intuitive Reiki For Our Times by Amy Z. Rowland

The Book on Karuna Reiki by Laurelle Gaia

The Seven Healing Chakras by Brenda Davies, M.D.

You Can Heal Your Life by Louise Hay

The Four Agreements by Don Miguel Ruiz

Be Here Now by Ram Dass

CDs/DVDs

Chakra Clearing (book and CD) by Doreen Virtue, PhD

The Reiki Touch (boxed set of book, CDs, and DVDs)
by William Lee Rand

Reiki Master Practicum (CD) Instruction by Laurelle Gaia

Infinite Spectrum (CD) Meditation by Laurelle Gaia

Reiki Chants (CD) Sound Healing by Jonathan Goldman

Acknowledgments

Heartfelt thanks and deep gratitude to everyone—the many teachers, guides, students, clients, friends, family members, readers, coaches, editors, and publishers—who helped me to realize my dream of writing this book. I couldn't have done it without you. Thank you.

About the Author

Deb Karpek is the owner of Peaceful World Reiki. Originally from Wisconsin, in 2012 she realized a dream and moved to northern Arizona, near Sedona, where she lives with her husband. She has been studying Reiki since 2001, practicing since 2003, and teaching since 2006. Deb is a Holy Fire II Usui and Karuna Reiki® Master/ Teacher, having received her Reiki certifications from the International Center for Reiki Training.

Deb received her Master of Spiritual Psychology from the School of Integrative Psychology In Glendale, WI and is certified as a Level 1 Breathwork Practitioner. She Is a Reiki Crystal Healer (Advanced Level), a Reiki Drum Practitioner, and a Reikisonics Sound Healer (Level One).

Deb is approved by the National Certification Board for Therapeutic Massage and Bodywork (NCBTMB) as a continuing education Approved Provider.

Having experienced profound life changes as a result of Reiki, Deb continues to study and practice the various modalities of energy medicine. She devotes her life to walking the Reiki path and helping others discover the benefits of Reiki.

For more information about the author, please visit
www.DebKarpek.com or Facebook.

CPSIA information can be obtained
at www.ICGtesting.com
Printed in the USA
FSOW04n2136110716
22606FS